The Tram... South

(Networks Edition)

This book, the sixteenth in our regional series, is based on Chapter 10 of *Great British Tramway Networks* by W.H.Bett and J.C.Gillham, published in its fourth edition in 1962 and long out of print. The building of railways during the middle years of the nineteenth century, from London outwards to the south coast, gave rise to the seaside resort and the need for links from the railway stations to the beach and town centres. These links were also needed in the naval port of Portsmouth and the growing commercial port of Southampton. This book charts the history of those tramways which existed between those covered in the *Tramways of Kent* and those covered in *The Tramways of South West England*. Unlike most other books in the series, each town developed its own system and there were no networks as such, and despite the efforts of the British Electric Traction Company many proposed tramways were never built.

We start our journey at Rye and then continue westwards along the coast through Hastings, Brighton, Portsmouth, and Southampton to Bournemouth. We also visit the Isle of Wight and conclude with an updated look at the new tramway at Seaton, some fifty miles to the west of Bournemouth, which has been further developed since our South West book in 1990.

Rye and Camber

Rye, sited on the River Rother, is an ancient town and one of the Cinque Ports, although its harbour is now two miles away. The Rye and Camber Tramway Company opened its line to the Camber Golf Links on 13 July 1895, and thirteen years later, on 13 July 1908, it was extended to Camber Sands. The two mile steam line was constructed to the three-foot gauge by Colonel H.F. Stephens of narrow-gauge railway fame. It was worked by two locomotives built by W.G.Bagnall, named Camber and Victoria, two coaches and three goods wagons. A Simplex tractor was obtained in later years.

In 1912 the journey from Rye to Camber Sands took fourteen minutes, with thirteen trips on weekdays, of which only seven went through to the Sands, the others terminating at the Golf Links. On Sundays there were only nine trips, five to the Sands and four to the Golf Links. In winter all services terminated at the Golf Links.

The Company was moderately prosperous, serving as it did a popular golf club and terminating among the sand dunes adjacent to a fine beach popular with holiday makers. The line was extended further along the sands in 1938 or 1939, but this was never used, as the whole line closed on the outbreak of war on 4 September 1939. It was taken over by the Admiralty in 1940, but was not re-opened after the war. The Company went into voluntary liquidation and the engines were scrapped in 1947.

Cover: **A scene at the Aquarium terminus in Brighton circa. 1930. No.52, built in 1914, and rebuilt in 1937, is seen in original condition with No.22, built in 1927, behind.**   (Painting by Ashley Best.

Hastings

The old town of Hastings, another of the Cinque Ports, is sited by the sea and developed mainly as a fishing port, while the new town developed later, out towards Bexhill, and on the hills rising, in places steeply, from the seashore.

No horse trams ever ran in Hastings, and it was not until 1897 that electric trams were proposed by a Mr. W.M.Murphy from Dublin, who successfully introduced trams in Paisley some years later. A further scheme was put forward in 1898 by the Provincial Tramways Company, through the Hastings, Bexhill and District Light Railways (Electric) Company Ltd.,which from 9 November 1904 became the Hastings and District Electric Tramways Company Ltd., when the Provincial sold their interest. The Company obtained two Acts. The first, the Hastings Tramways Act of 1900, authorised eight lines in Hastings. Also one in Bexhill from St.Leonards, (1¼ miles west of Hastings), to Cooden Beach was authorised by a Light Railway Order of 1900. The second Act, the Hastings Tramways (Extension) Act of 1903, authorised a connecting line along the Promenade providing overhead wires were not used.

The tram system as authorised, therefore, was in two parts, a 10½ mile town system in Hastings opened on 31 July 1905, and a lengthy route along the coast from St.Leonards through to Bexhill opened on 9 April 1906, and thence across the fields to Cooden Beach, opened on 28 July 1906. The two parts were finally linked on 12 January 1907 when the Promenade section from Hastings (Memorial) to St.Leonards, some two miles, was opened. Owing to the Borough Council's objection to overhead wires the Dolter surface-contact system was installed, but it was never really successful, as sand and sea water caused problems, and the last Dolter-equipped trams ran on 26 March 1914. The Dolter cars were converted to petrol-electric traction using the Tilling-Stevens system. A petrol engine, fitted under the stairs, drove a dynamo, fitted under a lower-saloon seat, which generated the electric current to drive the tram's motors. These trams lasted until 1920 when the Corporation relented and by Act of 1920 allowed overhead wires to be erected along 1¼ miles of the Promenade. Overhead electric traction was now used throughout the 19½ mile system, which was worked by 65 tramcars, all orthodox open-top four-wheelers, built at Preston, housed in two depots; Silverhill in Hastings and Bulverhythe in St.Leonards. A third, authorised at Ore, was never built.

The lengthy four-mile route along the coast linking Hastings with Bexhill was generally flat, with fine views of the sea from Hastings Promenade and Grand Parade. Beyond St.Leonards there was a half-mile length of reserved track before the descent of Manor Road into Bexhill. A further two miles of single line and five loops brought the trams to the terminus at Cooden Beach.

In contrast, the Hastings town system was generally hilly with a high proportion of single line and loop tracks. The principal service was a circular one of 8½ miles linking the town centre with Ore, St.Helens, Baldslow and Silverhill. There were steep gradients up to Ore, from where another steeply-graded line gave a link to the Old Town, and then to St.Helens 500 feet above sea level. Here on a clear day the trams offered fine views across the sea to Eastbourne, 13 miles, and inland across The Weald, nearly 20 miles, to the North Downs. They then continued on to Silverhill and down through Bohemia to the seafront. At Silverhill there was a line north to Hollington, and another one steeply down past Warrior Square Station to the sea at St.Leonards where a junction linked it to the Bexhill line at Grand Parade. Despite the steep hills there were no runaways.

The Albert Memorial was the centre of the Hastings Tramway system. No.2, showing Hollington on the rear screen, has presumably come via Bohemia and will run through to St.Helens Cemetery or reverse on the single-line off the picture and return to Hollington. (Judges card, courtesy Alan Brotchie

In the 1920's the Company proposed replacing its rather small old-fashioned cars by modern ones, but as the Corporation would offer no protection against the increasingly severe motor- bus competition, the Company decided to replace the trams by trolleybuses. The conversion duly took place over a thirteen month period, with the last tram running on 15 May 1929 from St.Helens to Silverhill. Maidstone & District Motor Services Ltd. took over control of the Hastings Company on 11 November 1935, and in 1967 it was merged with the M & D. The last trolleybus ran on 31 May 1959.

Electric traction also appeared briefly along a short length of The Promenade at the West Marina, St.Leonards, when two of the 15 in. gauge miniature trams, Nos.23 and 225, built by Claude Lane of Barnet, ran during the summer season of 1951.

Hastings Cliff Lifts

A half-mile tramway extension from the Albert Memorial to the Fish Market was authorised by Act of 1921, but not built. Hastings today has two cliff lifts, one about 300 yards west of the Fish Market and one about 300 yards to the east of it.

The West Cliff Lift was opened in 1891 by the Hastings Passenger Lift Company Ltd. and was taken over by Hastings Corporation in 1947. The 500 feet, (152 meters) lift, mostly in tunnel, has a gradient of 1 in 3, and a gauge of six feet. It was originally worked by a 40hp Crossley gas engine and since 1929 by a 32hp Tangye diesel engine. The two cars have seats for 12 passengers.

The steeper and shorter East Lift, in a cutting in the cliff face, was opened by the Corporation in 1903 and worked automatically on the water-balance principle, each car holding 600 gallons.

It is 267 feet (81 meters) long, with a gradient of 1 in 1.28 and a gauge of five feet. It closed in 1973 and re-opened three years later with electric operation. The original cars, seating 18, were replaced by new ones at the same time.

Eastbourne

The modern seaside resort of Eastbourne developed during the nineteenth century from the hamlets of East-Borne, South-Borne, and Sea Houses. Although it has 2½ miles of promenade and the railway station is half a mile from the sea it never had a tramway either in the town or to Beachy Head three miles to the south-west.

The nearest the town came to having a tramway was in 1885 when the Eastbourne & Pevensey Tramways Bill failed to pass standing orders. The Act would have authorised eight route miles of 3ft.6in. gauge, single-track with loops, of roadside steam tramway from Terminus Road, Eastbourne, along the main Hastings Road, A259 today, to Langney Bridge, and north through Langney and Westham to Pevensey, where it would have swung south to the sea and back on the B2191 along the edge of The Crumbles to rejoin the outward route at Langney Bridge.

Electric tramways for the town were proposed in 1899,1901 and 1902. In the latter year it was decided to appply for a Light Railway Order for four routes, totalling six miles, including one along Seaside Road, but this did not proceed despite a public meeting calling upon the Town Council to provide the town with a proper system of tramways. In 1903 the BET offered to install and work the tramway, but the offer was not accepted as the Council had opened the first municipal motor-bus service in Britain earlier in the year.

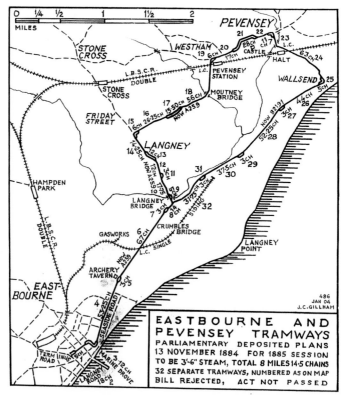

EASTBOURNE AND PEVENSEY TRAMWAYS
PARLIAMENTARY DEPOSITED PLANS
13 NOVEMBER 1884 FOR 1885 SESSION
TO BE 3'-6" STEAM, TOTAL 8 MILES 14·5 CHAINS
32 SEPARATE TRAMWAYS, NUMBERED AS ON MAP
BILL REJECTED, ACT NOT PASSED

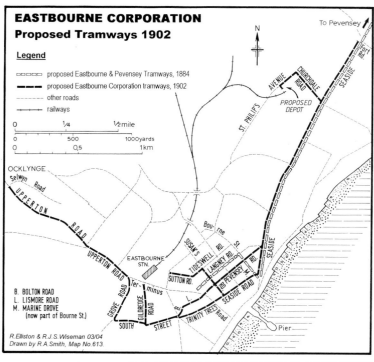

EASTBOURNE CORPORATION
Proposed Tramways 1902

Legend

- ▱▱▱▱▱ proposed Eastbourne & Pevensey Tramways, 1884
- ▬▬▬▬ proposed Eastbourne Corporation tramways, 1902
- ------ other roads
- ┼─┼─┼ railways

0	¼	½mile
0	500	1000yards
0	0,5	1km

To Pevensey

N

CHURCHDALE ROAD

AVENUE

ST. PHILIP'S

PROPOSED DEPOT

SEASIDE

Fort Rd.

OCKLYNGE

Selwyn Road

UPPERTON ROAD

UPPERTON ROAD

EASTBOURNE STN.

Ter-minus

SUSAN'S RD.

TIDESWELL RD.

LANCNEY RD.

PEVENSEY RD.

SEASIDE RD.

SEASIDE

Bou-rne St.

GROVE ROAD

GILDREDGE ROAD

SUTTON RD.

B.

L.

SEASIDE ROAD

M.

TRINITY TREES Road

SOUTH STREET

Pier

B. BOLTON ROAD
L. LISMORE ROAD
M. MARINE DROVE
(now part of Bourne St.)

R.Elliston & R.J.S.Wiseman 03/04
Drawn by R.A.Smith, Map No.613.

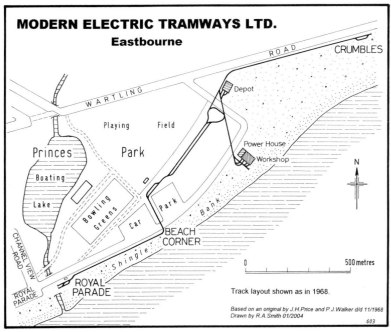

MODERN ELECTRIC TRAMWAYS LTD.
Eastbourne

ROAD

CRUMBLES

WARTLING

Playing   Field

Princes   Park

Boating

Lake

Bowling Greens

Car

Park

Bank

BEACH CORNER

Shingle

CHANNEL VIEW ROAD

ROYAL PARADE

ROYAL PARADE

Depot

Power House

Workshop

N

| 0 | 500 metres |

Track layout shown as in 1968.

Based on an original by J.H.Price and P.J.Walker d/d 11/1968
Drawn by R.A.Smith 01/2004

603

8

Electric traction finally came to Eastbourne in 1954 when Modern Electric Tramways Ltd., incorporated on 19 May 1953, opened the first 230 yards of two-foot gauge line to the Golf House at Whitsun, 4 July 1954. and to Princes Park Gates on 15 August 1954. The final extension to the Crumbles was opened on 24 May 1958. The open-top miniature trams were popular and the Company had hoped to extend the one-mile line further to Langney Point, but unfortunately the local council wanted to build a new road across the Crumbles and so the tramway operated for the last time on 14 September 1969. The seven trams were transferred to the Seaton Tramway in Devon.

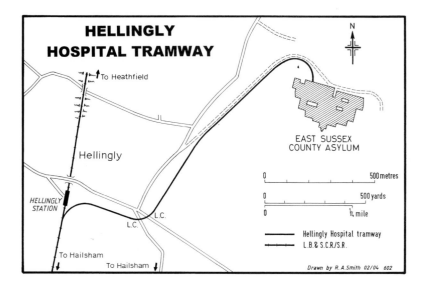

Hellingly Hospital

Eight miles north of Eastbourne is Hellingly, which once had a station on the London Brighton and South Coast Railway line from Eridge to Polegate. From a point just south of the station an electric tramway ran 1.15 miles east and then north-east to Hellingly Hospital. The line had railway-type track and tramway-type poles and bracket arms for the overhead wire. It was opened on 20 July 1903 and conveyed passengers until 25 March 1959 and coal until 1961. The electric locomotive was supplied by R.Blackwell & Co.Ltd., and the electric tramcar, almost certainly built by Brush, ran until 1931.

Newhaven

Linked to London by rail, Newhaven sited on the mouth of the River Ouse, is a seaside town with ferry links across the Channel to Dieppe. In 1884 the Brighton and South Coast Tramways Bill was promoted to construct a steam tramway of 9.3 miles from Newhaven to Brighton Aquarium. This failed, but was revived the following year for a line a mile shorter, curtailed at the Newhaven end and terminating at Kemp Town railway station. The line would have been hilly with a maximum gradient of 1 in 15.5 through sparsely populated country, but the Bill did not proceed.

Passengers enjoy a trip on Volk's sea-going tram 'Daddy Long-legs'.
(Steugel card, courtesy National Tramway Museum)

Brighton and Rottingdean

This unique line, known colloquially as "Daddy Long-legs", was opened on 28 November 1896 and ran from the eastern side of Banjo Groyne to Rottingdean, the proposed terminus five years later of the Beach Railway. The two parallel tracks of 2ft.8½ in. gauge, with their inner rails set 12ft.7in. apart, were laid on concrete blocks at roughly low-tide level. Construction was by the British Thomson-Houston Company Ltd. Piers were provided at Banjo Groyne and Rottingdean, with a landing stage at Ovingdean Gap about halfway along the three-mile line.

The single saloon car, 50ft. long by 22ft. wide, was supported on four legs 23ft. long, enough to give the car clearance above the waves at high tide. The car carried a lifeboat to comply with Board of Trade requirements. There were four trucks, with 33-inch wheels, one at the foot of each leg. Power was from overhead wires suspended alongside the track. This was fed through two 25hp motors on two of the legs to the trucks. The other two legs carried the brake rigging.

At high tide some 16 feet of water covered the rails and the car moved through it at about 5 m.p.h., the journey taking a little over half an hour. Unfortunately the line did not survive the British weather. On 4 December 1896, only four days after opening, severe gales tore the car from its moorings and damaged the tracks. It re-opened on 20 July 1897 following repairs, but Brighton Corporation gave three months notice on 1 September 1900 that the rails would have to be moved further out to sea to allow two groynes protecting the shore to be extended. As it would have been impossible to move the car through a greater depth of water the line was abandoned in February 1901.

The two ex-Southend Pier cars, Nos.8 and 9, leave the Aquarium terminus of Volks
Electric Railway on 2 May 1974.   (J.H.Price, courtesy National Tramway Museum.

Volks Railway, Brighton

The other railway enterprise of Magnus Volk on the east side of Brighton needs to be recorded. The first to be built, the first public electric railway anywhere in Britain, was the two-foot gauge Beach Electric Railway which was opened on 4 August 1883 along the beach from the Palace Pier to the old Chain Pier. It was extended eastwards on 4 April 1884 to Banjo Groyne, reconstructed on 2ft.8½ in. gauge with a centre conductor rail, and finally extended to the present terminus at Black Rock on 21 February 1901. A further planned 1901 extension to Rottingdean was never built. After the 1914-18 War it was cut back at the Brighton end from the Palace Pier to a new station some 200 metres to the east. Single-deck cars are used, with four-car sets at peak times. It ran throughout the year, unless closed due to storm damage, until wartime closure on 2 July 1940, and re-opened on 15 May 1948 following renovation. Since 1954 the line has been operated during the summer season only, generally from mid-March until the end of September. Magnus Volk died on 20 May 1937 and on 1 April 1939 his family sold the railway to Brighton Corporation, which still operates it today.

Brighton

Situated only 51 miles from London by rail Brighton, originally the village of Brighthelmstone, became popular after the then Prince of Wales, later King George IV, spent a holiday there in 1782, and two years later started to build the Royal Pavilion. This was finished in 1827 and purchased by the town in 1849 and is now a concert hall and museum. The town prospered as a seaside resort for Londoners after the opening of the railway in 1841.

The town developed in its cup-like depression in the South Downs through which ran the road and railway from London with steep hills rising over 400 feet to the east and the north. To the west, through Hove to beyond Shoreham, there was a flat coastal plain. Despite the hills and the narrow main streets, St.James Street eastwards and North Street westwards, both unsuitable for tramways, a Bill for 8.3 miles of tramway was proposed in

A scene at St. Peter's Church, Brighton. No.29 is heading north from Grand Parade while No. 15 will continue via Gloucester Place round the town centre loop.
(Mezzotint card, courtesy A.W. Brotchie.

1872 and included a main line from Kemp Town via the promenades to Southwick Harbour. Unfortunately the Bill failed owing to opposition to the line along the promenades.

No further Bills were promoted until 1884, when the Brighton & District Tramways Company, which had opened the Shoreham tramway on 3 July, promoted the Brighton District Extension Bill with the aim of linking its Shoreham Line with Brighton, but owing to the opposition of Hove the Bill failed to pass through Parliament.

Electric tramways were first proposed in 1900 when Brighton Corporation obtained powers to build seven miles of line. Further Acts in 1902 and 1903 authorised extensions totalling 2.5 miles. Construction started almost immediately and the first route, along the Lewes Road, opened with due ceremony on 25 November 1901. Construction continued apace and all authorised routes were built by July 1904 except for a direct line from Seven Dials to the Station. A Light Railway Act in 1919 authorised an extension of the Lewes Road route to serve the Moulsecoomb housing estate, but this was never built.

Owing to the many narrow streets Brighton's tramways were built to the narrower 3ft. 6in. gauge, and 166 open-top tramcars were owned over the years, with a maximum of 80 at any one time.The first 40 were built by Milnes, then ten by UEC, and all there-after in the well-equipped Corporation workshops. They were kept in excellent condition and continually updated. Most of the older equipments were replaced by new, and new bodies were built as late as 1937.

The hub of the Brighton system was Aquarium terminus, approached until 1929 by an anti-clockwise one-way system round the Old Steine Gardens, but clockwise thereafter, close by the Palace Pier and the sea front. From this point trams ran inland to the Central Station, Dyke Road, Beaconsfield Road, Ditchling Road, Lewes Road and via Elm Grove to Race Hill. The Dyke Road, Ditchling Road with short lengths at 1 in 9, and Elm Grove routes were steeply inclined, and from these termini there were panoramic views of the coast and English Channel. Trams on the Queens Park route had to reverse from Elm Grove into Queens Park Road to continue down hill to the terminus at St.James Street. Unfortunately the short distance along St.James Street to the Old Steine was never worked by trams, although later by trolleybuses.

HOVE and SHOREHAM Tramways

Legend

- Brighton & Shoreham Tramways Company Ltd., as built
- Brighton & Shoreham Tramways Co. Ltd., authorised, not built
- Brighton Corporation Tramways, as built
- Brighton Corporation Tramways, authorised, not built
- Brighton Street Tramways Co., proposed (1872), not authorised
- Hove & Worthing Electric Tramways Ltd., authorised, not built
- Hove Corporation Tramways, proposed (1902), not authorised
- other roads
- Brighton – Hove boundary
- railways

Hove Corporation and Hove & Worthing data based on J.C. Gillham's map No 211, d/d 01/1957. Brighton & Shoreham data based on W.J Wyse's map d/d 07/65. Much additional data from N.Kellett. Drawn by R.A.Smith, August, 2004. Map N°. 632

N

BRIGHTON CENTRAL STN.

SEVEN DIALS

Brighton

To Kemp Town

West Pier

KINGS ROAD

DYKE RD.

York Rd.

WESTERN RD.

HOLLAND RD. HALT

HOLLAND ROAD

DAVIGDOR ROAD

ROAD

KINGSWAY

CROM-WELL ROAD

DENMARK VILLAS

VENTNOR VILLAS

HOVE STN.

CLARMONT VILLAS

GOLDSTONE VILLAS

Hove

CHURCH ROAD

ALDRINGTON STN.

ROAD

UPPER WESTBOURNE VILLAS

ROAD

CHURCH ROAD

KINGSWAY

NEW

Portslade by Sea

PORTSLADE STN.

PORTLAND RD.

BOUNDARY RD.

STATION RD.

ST. ANDREW'S RD.

1 mile

3/4

1/2

1/4

1000 yards

500

1 km

0,5

0

FISHERGATE STN.

CHURCH RD.

ST. ANDREW'S RD.

ANDREW'S ST.

EASTBROOK RD.

MILL RD.

WELLINGTON RD.

FISHERGATE TERRACE

Leylands

Gardner Rd.

STREET

Coastguard Stn.

SOUTHWICK STN.

Southwick

Depot

Shoreham Harbour

ALBION ST.

ALBION RD.

Lighthouse

BRIGHTON ROAD

Malthouse

Station Rd.

Butts Rd.

Depot

Shoreham by Sea

SHOREHAM STN.

WR. HAM RD.

HAM RD.

LOWER BRIGHTON ROAD

HIGH ST.

SOUTH-DOWN RD.

SE. HR.

WR.

B. BRUNSWICK RD.
HR. HEBE RD.
SG. SWISS GARDENS
WR. WESTERN RD.

River Adur

To South Lancing (Worthing Borough boundary)

Brighton's trams operated profitably for nearly forty years until replaced, except for Dyke Road, by trolleybuses during 1939 under a co-ordination agreement with the Brighton, Hove and District Omnibus Company Ltd. The last tram, No.41, running from Queens Park, entered Lewes Road depot early on 1 September 1939.

Hove

Hove, a municipal borough, continues the Brighton built-up area westwards towards Shoreham. As already noted Hove would not agree to the Shoreham tramway being extended through Hove to Brighton, and this attitude persisted throughout the tramway era. A Tramway Bill was however deposited in December 1902 for electric tramways, in response to the British Electric Traction Company's Hove, Worthing & District proposals, and in view of its Tramways Act, powers to acquire that small portion of the Brighton and Shoreham horse line which lay within its area. The Bill proposed 4.25 miles of 3ft. 6in. gauge, mainly double-track, line linking Seven Dials across Hove to the Shoreham line, plus branches, and Brighton laid a spur at Seven Dials into Goldsmid Road to connect with this proposal, but a poll of residents and ratepayers produced an adverse vote and the failure of the Bill the following spring.

One of the double-deck cars, Nos.5(ii)-9(ii) is seen at the Burrell Arms, terminus of the Brighton and Shoreham tramway. Shoreham station is to the right of the level crossing.
(Staffords Bazaar, Brighton, courtesy National Tramway Museum.)

The nearest Hove got to electric public transport was an Act in 1912 for 8.25 miles of trolleybus route, and trolleybus demonstrations in 1912 and 1914. The first was a Ransomes vehicle on London Road, and the second a Cedes-Stoll trolleybus which ran between Hove Station and Hove Town Hall via George Street from 16 September 1914 until 9 August 1915.

Shoreham

Shoreham sited at the mouth of the River Adur, some six miles west of Brighton, is a small port importing mainly coal for the local area, and for power stations. Here, the first tramway in the Brighton district, was authorised by the Brighton District Tramways Act, 1882. The Brighton District Tramways Company duly constructed 4.64 miles of the 5.39 miles authorised. The main line, 4.15 miles of 3ft. 6in. gauge single track with 15 loops, ran from Shoreham LBSCR Station along the coast road through Southwick to Portslade, where it turned north onto Station Road before continuing east to the Hove boundary. This opened on 3 July 1884, with steam traction except for the western end beyond Shoreham Station, 0.49 miles, which was horse-operated and soon abandoned as steam was not authorised here.

Steam traction was not successful on the rest of the route, the engines possibly being too heavy for the track, and horse traction was introduced in 1885 to supplement the steam trams. However the company was not a financial success and went into liquidation in 1888, and a new company, the Brighton and District Tramway Company Ltd., took over the concern. It abandoned steam altogether, but was unable to make a profit and followed its predecessor into liquidation in May 1889.

A fresh start was made in November 1889 when a further new company, the Brighton and Shoreham Tramways Company Ltd., took over the line. This Company was acquired by the British Electric Traction Company Ltd. in June 1898, who planned to rebuild and electrify the line, and extend it eastwards to Brighton and westwards to Worthing. A scheme eastwards to link it with Brighton in 1901 was barred by Hove, as had been that of the original company in 1883. Two schemes to extend the tramway westward into Worthing were put forward in 1902 and 1903. Although the B.E.T. received partial sanction nothing was done, nor did a Brighton District Tramways Bill of 1911 go forward. The horse tramway continued to operate until 1912, when Hove's Act to introduce trolleybuses also authorised it to remove the rails from New Church Road, Aldrington, by now incorporated into the Borough of Hove. The whole line was officially abandoned in October 1912, except that one car continued to run until 6 June 1913.

Devil's Dyke

A huge natural fissure in the north-facing chalk escarpment of the South Downs some 4½ miles north-west of Brighton, the Devil's Dyke is a ravine cutting into the Downs, which rise here to 700 feet above sea level and give exceptional views over a wide area. To cater for visitors an LBSCR branch railway ran from Hove to the southern foot of The Dyke from 1 September 1887 until 31 December 1938. To save the steep climb on the north side the Brighton Dyke Steep Grade Railway Co., Ltd. built a funicular railway from

Tram No.10, cut down to single-deck in 1908, is seen on the loop in Fishergate Terrace on the last day of operation, 6 June 1913.

(Courtesy National Tramway Museum.

the village of Poynings up the north-facing escarpment. The 840-foot long line of three-foot gauge, powered by a Hornsby Ackroyd oil engine, rose 395 feet in three sections with gradients of 1 in 2.9, 1 in 1.5, and 1 in 1.8 respectively. The two cars, built by Ashbury, seated fourteen passengers and ran at 3 mph. The line was opened on 24 July 1897 and closed in 1908, with most of the equipment removed by 1913.

There was also a 1,200 foot long aerial cableway stretching across the ravine itself, with an endless cable powered by a Crossley oil engine, and two cars each seating four passengers. This opened on 13 October 1894 and closed in 1909.

Worthing

Three hundred years ago Worthing was a fishing hamlet, the nearest village being Broadwater, with a church dating back to Saxon times, 1½ miles inland. A toll bridge constructed across the River Adur at Shoreham, also the turnpike road in 1832, and the railway westwards from Brighton built in 1845, all improved access and the town developed as a select seaside resort. It achieved Borough status in 1890 and owned a municipal power station from 1901.

Between 1901 and 1911 there were six tramway schemes in the Worthing area. The first was the Corporation scheme of 1901, which envisaged almost nine miles of line, much of it north of the railway in open country to Findon, nestling in the Downs. Despite much debate, or maybe because of it, no Light Railway Order was applied for. Second was the 1902 B.E.T. scheme, to electrify the Shoreham horse tramway and extend it eastwards to Seven Dials, Brighton, via Hove Station and westwards via Norfolk Bridge and Lancing to Worthing, with a loop system within the town. This failed due to the opposition of Worthing Corporation.

Two further revised schemes then followed. Thus the Council proposed a town scheme and the BET proposed 22 miles of tramway connecting Brighton with Littlehampton, eight miles to the west of Worthing. An agreement was eventually reached and both Bills went before Parliament early in 1903. Both received the Royal Assent on 11 August 1903. The Worthing Corporation Tramways Act authorised 7.90 miles linking Worthing with Lancing and Broadwater, while the Hove, Worthing & District Tramways Act, omitting the Littlehampton portion, authorised the BET to build 4.81 miles of new tramway, and it registered the Hove & Worthing Electric Tramways Limited to do this. Owing to Council opposition nothing was done and the powers lapsed in August 1910.

A year later, the Brighton District Tramways proposed building a line from Seven Dials, Brighton, to Steyne Gardens, Worthing, via a reconstructed horse tramway. This failed due to official opposition, as did a second Brighton District scheme soon afterwards. Promoted by George Balfour and A.H. Beatty, this sought to take over the lapsed BET powers.

Littlehampton

Sited on the River Arun, half-a-mile inland from the coast, Littlehampton is a small port with a safe harbour. It is also a seaside resort with a fine beach and a golf course. Even though the population was only some 7,000 an electric tramway of 3ft. 6in. gauge and one mile in length was applied for by Magnus Volk and others in November 1886. It would have linked the railway station with a proposed new pier via Terminus Road, High Street, South Street and Beach Road. The scheme was rejected after a public inquiry chaired by Major General Hutchinson, held on 17 March 1887, on the ground that the Board of Trade knew insufficient about electric traction in the streets. After all, Blackpool had opened only 2½ years earlier.

16

As already noted, the B.E.T. proposed a through tramway from Littlehampton to Brighton in 1903. This would have started outside Littlehampton Station and followed Volk's proposed line to the beach; thence eastwards along the Esplanade, about one mile to its end, where a depot was planned. Here it would have continued on private track behind the sea wall, single line with numerous passing loops for about five miles to West Worthing, through open country, remote from the six villages which lay half a mile inland. Although the B.E.T. was successful in obtaining powers elsewhere the Littlehampton section was omitted from its 1903 Act.

All the schemes, except for those in the Brighton area, on this part of the South Coast, fell by the wayside due in part to the negative attitude of some of the local authorities. If all had been built it would have been possible to travel by tram from Newhaven via Brighton, Hove, Shoreham and Worthing to Littlehampton, a distance of almost thirty miles. In 1900 the towns, except for Brighton, were small with considerable open country between. To-day this part of the Sussex coast is almost continuously built up and the proposed tramway would no doubt be flourishing. The coast to-day is, however, well-served by electric trains and buses.

Selsey

The Hundred of Manhood & Selsey Tramways Co.Ltd., incorporated on 29 April 1896, was legally a tramway although more of a light railway in appearance, being a standard-gauge line across rural fields. Its engineer and later the chairman was Lt.Col. H.F.Stephens of Tonbridge. It opened on 27 August 1897 and ran from Chichester LBSCR Station southwards 7¾ miles to Selsey Beach. An Act of 1924 changed the legal, but not trading, name to West Sussex Railway Company. It escaped the grouping in 1921 and remained independent until abandoned on 19 January 1935.

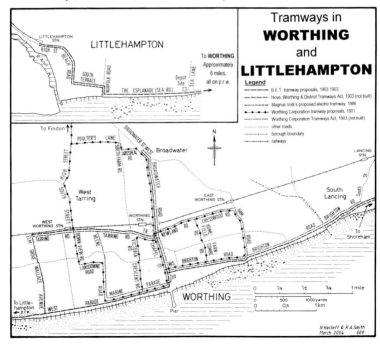

There were seven locomotives at various times, but never more than four at once. It opened with three Falcon bogie tramcars and one by Hurst Nelson, later augmented by nine mixed secondhand coaches. In 1913 there were eleven journeys per day, but only six by 1934, provided from 1929 onwards mostly by two pairs of back-to-back petrol railcars.

Hayling Island

Separated from Portsmouth by Langstone Harbour, Hayling Island is mainly a residential and holiday area, with most housing extending some three miles along the Channel coast. It lies south of Havant on the LBSCR Brighton-Portsmouth line which opened in 1847, but the Hayling Railway Company did not complete the branch to South Hayling until 16 July 1867.

The Portsmouth and Hayling Light Railway Order was confirmed by the Board of Trade on 29 March 1905 and authorised construction of a tramway from South Hayling to the pumping station at Eastney, 3.96 miles, including a conveyor transporter suspension bridge 1056 feet in length across the entrance to Langstone Harbour. At Eastney Portsmouth Corporation would have extended their tramway from Highland Road to the pumping station and leased it to the Hayling Island. However, although an extension of time was granted on 11 November 1910, nothing was done. Doubtless the cost of the bridge deterred the investors.

The South Hayling railway branch closed on 4 November 1963 and a year later efforts were made by the Hayling Light Railway Society to re-open it as an electric light railway. Although the Havant and Hayling Island Rapid Transit Company was formed, the project did not proceed. The only evidence was the arrival of Blackpool Car No.11 in 1965. This tram is now restored and located at Carlton Colville.

Portsdown No.5 on street track at Waterlooville en-route to Cosham circa 1910. The through service to Portsmouth was not introduced until 1924.
(Wrench series, courtesy National Tramway Museum.

Portsdown and Horndean

A glance at the railway map of Southern England will show that there was a gap in north-south connections to the coast between Havant and Fareham. This gap in transport facilities was exploited by the Hampshire Light Railways (Electric) Company Limited, which built a tramway from Cosham, where it connected with the Portsmouth Corporation tramways, to Horndean.

The Portsmouth Street Tramways Company's horse tramway was extended in 1881 beyond the then city boundary to Cosham Railway Station. In 1884 an Act was obtained to extend it through Cosham, but this was not built, nor was its proposed extension up Portsdown Hill and as a roadside line to Waterlooville. As the later compulsory purchase by Portsmouth Corporation would have left the Company with only the outer end of their line, Hilsea to Cosham, it was decided in 1897 that the Hampshire Company, formed then by the Provincial Group, would build the electric tramway to Horndean.

Construction began in January 1902, and the line was opened with a procession of six cars on 2 March 1903. The light railway left Cosham on private ballasted sleeper track, and bridged the main-line railway and two roads before climbing Portsdown Hill, alongside but above the road. It was then single line and loops to the terminus, which was some distance short of the village. Beyond Waterlooville it ran on private ballasted track on the east side of the A3 trunk road. It had originally been intended to extend the line through Horndean to Petersfield, seven miles, and build a branch from Waterlooville to Hambledon via Denmead, 4½ miles.

The initial service was from Cosham Interchange Platform, with some Corporation cars running to the top of Portsdown Hill. These unremunerative runs ended on 30 June 1907. A through service of Company cars to Portsmouth Town Hall was introduced on 1 August 1924, and was extended in stages to South Parade Pier, reached on 19 April 1927. To run this service there was a total of 23 open-top trams, including 16 from 1903-05, and seven from the associated Fareham company in 1930, also an 'open boat' from Grimsby, another Provincial Company.

Conversion of the last Portsmouth-Cosham tram service to trolleybus operation on 1 October 1934 meant that the through Portsdown-Horndean service could no longer continue, so the tramway service from Portsmouth-was abandoned on 9 January 1935 and replaced by Southdown motor buses. The Horndean trams had run through open country for much of their journey. To-day residental development is almost continuous from Cosham to Horndean and would surely benefit from the introduction of a modern tramway.

Portsmouth

The history of Portsmouth goes back to 1194 when Richard Coeur-de-Lion granted its first charter. Situated on Portsea Island and until 1940 linked to the mainland by only a single bridge at Hilsea, it became a County Borough in 1889 and a City in 1927. Including Southsea, its suburbs now extend well beyond Portsea Island to the slopes of Portsdown Hill. Portsmouth has a fine natural harbour and developed as a naval base with large dockyards. Portsmouth also operated tramcars on the unusual 4ft. 7¾ in. gauge continuously from 1865 until 1936. Now, after a gap of almost seventy years, it is hoped trams will run again to Portsmouth and Southsea station, this time on one mile of standard-gauge tracks, with a tunnel under the harbour from Gosport.

Four separate companies operated horse tramways in Portsmouth. First was the Landport and Southsea Tramways Company which obtained a private Act in 1863.

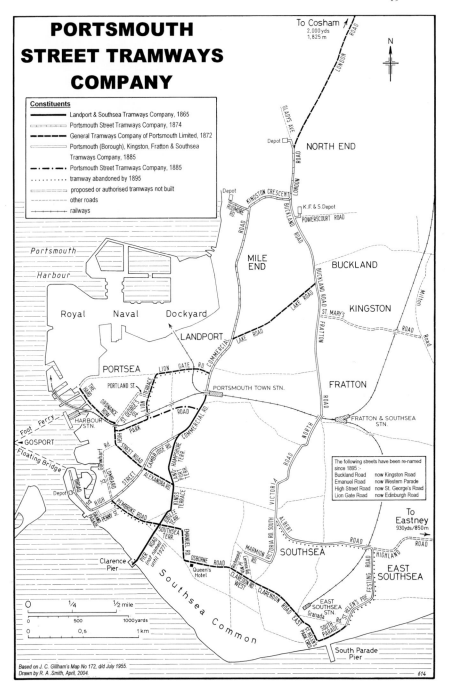

PORTSMOUTH STREET TRAMWAYS COMPANY

Constituents

————	Landport & Southsea Tramways Company, 1865
▭▭▭▭	Portsmouth Street Tramways Company, 1874
▬ ▬ ▬ ▬	General Tramways Company of Portsmouth Limited, 1872
═══════	Portsmouth (Borough), Kingston, Fratton & Southsea Tramways Company, 1885
—·—·—·	Portsmouth Street Tramways Company, 1885
·········	tramway abandoned by 1895
═══▷	proposed or authorised tramways not built
——————	other roads
┼─┼─┼─┼	railways

To Cosham
2,000 yds
1,825 m

N

LONDON ROAD

GLADYS AVE

Depot

NORTH END

UNION ROAD

Depot

KINGSTON CRESCENT

RUDMORE RD

ROAD

BUCKLAND ROAD

K.F. & S.Depot

POWERSCOURT ROAD

MILE END

BUCKLAND

BUCKLAND ROAD

KINGSTON

Milton

Road

LAKE ROAD

ST. MARY'S

FRATTON

ROAD

Portsmouth Harbour

Harbour

Royal   Naval   Dockyard

LANDPORT

LAKE ROAD

COMMERCIAL

PORTSEA

LION   GATE   RD.

PORTLAND ST.

ORDNANCE ROW

ST. GEORGE'S

LION TERRACE

ROAD

PARK

PORTSMOUTH TOWN STN.

COMMERCIAL RD

HAMPSHIRE TERR.

LAND PORT TERR.

FRATTON

FRATTON & SOUTHSEA STN.

NORTH

ROAD

HARBOUR STN.

Foot Ferry

GOSPORT

Floating Bridge

THE HARD

GUNWHARF RD.

HIGH STREET ROAD

CAMBRIDGE RD

ALEXANDRA RD.

KING'S TERRACE

VICTORIA RD SOUTH

LOMBARD ST.

HIGH STREET

PEMBROKE ROAD

JUBILEE TERR.

SOUTHSEA TERR.

EMANUEL RD.

OSBORNE ROAD

PALMERSTON RD

VICTORIA ROAD SOUTH

ALBERT ROAD

The following streets have been re-named since 1895 :-
Buckland Road   now Kingston Road
Emanuel Road   now Western Parade
High Street Road now St. George's Road
Lion Gate Road   now Edinburgh Road

To Eastney
930yds/850m

ROAD

HIGHLAND

ROAD

SOUTHSEA

EAST SOUTHSEA

FESTING ROAD

Depot

BROAD ST.

PENNY ST.

PIER ROAD (re-named until 1921)

Clarence Pier

Southsea   Common

MARMION RD.

LENNOX RD.

Queen's Hotel

CLARENDON RD WEST

CLARENDON ROAD EAST

ST HELEN'S PDE

EAST SOUTHSEA STN.

Granada

SOUTH PARADE RD.

ST. HELEN'S PDE

ST. PAUL'S CRES

South Parade Pier

0	¼	½ mile	
0	500	1000 yards	
0	0,5	1 km	

Based on J. C. Gillham's Map No 172, d/d July 1955.
Drawn by R. A .Smith, April, 2004.

614

High Street, Portmouth, showing the interlaced track at the Broad Street end. Tramcar No. 37 is heading north.

(Barkshire Bros, courtesy A.W. Brotchie.

This was the first Act to be passed authorising an English tramway company to build and operate tramways in the town. The first route, from the station to Southsea Pier, opened on 15 May 1865. The Portsmouth Street Tramways Company, a subsidiary of the Provincial Tramways Company Limited, was formed in 1873 and opened a line from the Floating Bridge to North End on 11 September 1874. The General Tramways Company of Portsmouth Ltd. opened a route on 18 March 1878 from the Floating Bridge to the Queens Hotel, Southsea. Finally the Portsmouth (Borough), Kingston, Fratton and Southsea Tramways Company obtained an Act in 1882, and on 26 November 1885 opened its route from Fratton Bridge to East Southsea.

All these companies eventually came under the control of the Provincial Company, the first three in 1883 and the PBKFS in 1892. At its maximum the Provincial used 65 trams on twelve miles of route. Its most interesting item of rolling stock was LIFU, a double-deck unit using paraffin to heat its boiler. The flue chimney passed through the knifeboard seat and roof on the top deck. It ran from 1896 to 1901 from the Town Hall to North End and ended its days as an office at Cowplain depot on the Horndean line. The Company promoted the Portsmouth Street Tramways Bill to electrify in 1896, but in the end the system was taken over by Portsmouth Corporation on 1 January 1901.

The Corporation duly electrified and extended the tramway system. The first electric car, No.1, ran from North End Depot to Clarence Pier on 24 September 1901, and extensions were built out to Alexandra Park, Copnor, Milton and Eastney. These routes were served by a fleet of 96 open-top single-truck cars built at Preston, some later rebuilt, and four converted horse trams. A single-deck toastrack tram from Southampton was added in 1919 and this ran as a tourist car from time to time. Twelve totally enclosed cars came in 1920, then in October 1930 a new improved totally enclosed tram appeared on the streets, but sadly, as in many other towns, it was the only one, and was sold to

The horse tram terminus at Gosport Hard. The fare on the ferry to Portsmouth Station, visible in the distance, was one penny.

(Wrench series, courtesy A.W. Brotchie.

Sunderland where it ran until 1953. Improvements were made to the track layout in later years, including reserved tracks from Ports Bridge to Cosham turning circle, and a new depot and works opened at Eastney on 21 January 1932.

The Fawcett Road route was the first abandonment, on 19 April 1931, but the remaining routes were mostly converted to trolleybus operation between 4 August 1934 and 10 November 1936, when the last tram, No.106, ran from the Guildhall to Eastney. One tram, ex-horse car No.84, was retained as a museum piece and is now in the new Hampshire Museum at Basingstoke.

Gosport and Fareham

Gosport is a market town and port on the west side of Portsmouth Harbour, and its industries were associated with ships and yachts. The Gosport Street Tramways Company, a subsidiary of the Provincial Tramways Company, obtained an Act in 1879, but construction was not started until 1882. The horse-operated three-foot gauge tramway from Gosport Hard to Ann's Hill opened on 17 July 1882 and was extended to Brockhurst early in 1883. In August 1883 the Company was amalgamated with the other Portsmouth companies into the Portsmouth Street Tramways Company. The Gosport, Alverstoke and Bury Cross Tramways Company, possibly a subsidiary of the Portsmouth Company, planned 2.45 miles of three-foot gauge track between these points, but the work was never started.

Under Acts of 1901,1903 and 1905 the Brockhurst horse tramway was reconstructed for electric traction and extended to Fareham, with a new line from Gosport to Bury Cross. These were built to the 4ft. 7¾ in. gauge, totalled 7.75 miles, and opened on 24 January and 13 October 1906 respectively. The tracks in Gosport and Fareham towns were double, linked by roadside sleeper track with passing loops along the west side of the A32 road, and were served by a fleet of 22 open-top trams from Brush and Milnes Voss.

The lines to Alverstoke, authorised in 1901, were never built: nor was the line authorised in 1903 from Fareham to Cosham. Here this would have linked with the Portsdown and Horndean Light Railway, which company tried in 1910 for the same line to Fareham. Finally application in November 1910 for a Gosport and Lee-on-the-Solent Light Railway Order, for a line 2½ miles from Bury Cross, was not granted, and the Company ran a motor bus service instead.

The Fareham tramway served the public for almost 24 years, being abandoned during 1929, the last section, Ann's Hill to Gosport, on 31 December. The tramway, although trading as Gosport and Fareham Tramways, was owned by the Portsmouth Street Tramways Company, which was authorised by its Act of 1929 to abandon the tramways, run motor buses, and change its name to the Gosport and Fareham Omnibus Company.

Haslar Hospital Tramway

The imposing Naval Hospital close by the Gosport shore of Spithead was for about fifty years linked by a short 400-yard standard-gauge tramway with the jetty. The tram which conveyed the patients to the hospital entrance was built by the Midland Railway Carriage and Wagon Company of Saltley in 1877 and propelled by naval personnel when required. There was also about 1¼ miles of narrow-gauge goods tramway, interlacing in part with the above, extending to Fort Blockhouse and Fort Monckton.

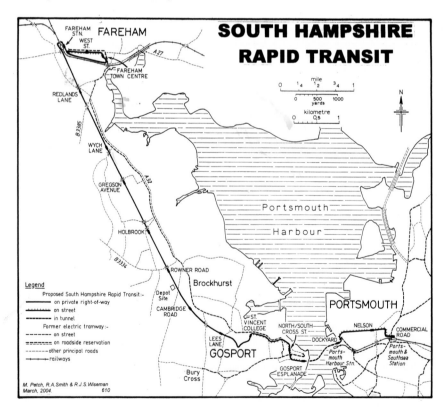

South Hampshire Rapid Transit

The Fareham tramway, as did Horndean, ran through open country for much of its length. Since abandonment there has been considerable residental development, and the need for an improved transport link to Portsmouth is vital. This new link, it is hoped, will be a modern 6½ mile tramway from Portsmouth city centre to Fareham, starting at Portsmouth and Southsea Station, then via Commercial Road and Edinburgh Road, with a tunnel beneath the sea channel before following for some distance the trackbed of the former railway line from Gosport to Fareham.

Isle of Wight

This picturesque island of 147 square miles with spectacular chalk cliffs, including the Needles off the west coast, is popular with holiday makers and therefore has a number of holiday resorts, several of which were the subject of tramway schemes that never got beyond the drawing board. To reach the island three ferries operated, one from Southampton (Royal Pier) to Cowes, one from Southsea (Clarence Pier) to Ryde, and a third from Lymington to Yarmouth which started later.

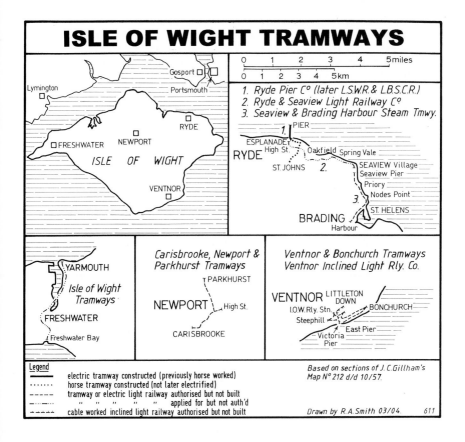

Ryde Pier

To reach deep water at all stages of the tide, a pier 1,704 feet long, later 2,250 feet, was opened in 1814. On this pier a standard-gauge horse tramway was opened by the Ryde Pier Company in 1864 and was extended in 1871 about one mile through the streets of the town to the then railway terminus at St.John's Road, but this extension was replaced by a railway extension in 1880. The Pier Tramway was electrified on the third-rail system in 1886, with one electrified horse tram plus two trailers working on each line of the double track. In October 1927 the Southern Railway, by now the owners of the track, replaced electric traction with two Drewry petrol railcars and ex-electric trailers. The tramway was closed on 26 January 1969, being replaced by ex-London Transport tube trains on the adjacent railway pier. Trailer No.4, erroneously numbered 3, of 1871, is in the Hull Transport Museum, and an 1889 Pollard electric car is preserved on the Island.

The Ryde and Seaview Light Railway Company applied in 1899 for 2¾ miles of 3ft. 6in. gauge electric tramway from the Esplanade via High Street and along the coast at Spring Vale to Seaview Village. This would have linked with the nearby standard-gauge Seaview and Brading Harbour Steam Tramway, authorised in 1882. which was to connect Seaview Pier with St.Helens and Brading Harbour, 1.90 miles to the south.

Ventnor

Ventnor is built in terraces up the chalk hillside, rising to well over 700 feet in St. Boniface Down, under which the Isle of Wight Railway from Shanklin came in tunnel to the eastern of two stations at about 350 feet above the town centre and its beaches. In 1864 the Ventnor Tramway Company proposed a steam tramway from this station down to Belgrave Road, zig-zagging with one reversal so as to ease the gradient. A year later this was again asked for, and granted, now extended down to the East Pier, via Bonchurch with two more reversals, as the Ventnor and Bonchurch Tramway, but this was not built. Neither was the Ventnor Inclined Light Railway, which Company applied in 1898 for a cable-operated line of 5ft. 9in. gauge, in three sections, with two cars on each, from the sea-front near the pier to the top of Littleton Downs 598 feet higher. Only the two lower sections, to the eastern railway station, were authorised, these in 1899.

Newport

The Isle of Wight Tramways Company proposed in 1879 a street tramway from Carisbrooke to Newport Railway Station, 1¼ miles, which also failed. This was revived and extended ten years later as the Carisbrooke, Newport and Parkhurst Tramways, 2¼ miles, to run from Carisbrooke Church via Newport High Street to the gates of Parkhurst Prison. Sadly the prisoners never had the chance to leave by tram.

Yarmouth

On the far west of the island, failed to get a horse tramway proposed by this same Isle of Wight Tramways Company in 1879. This would have run from Yarmouth Pier along the east side of the Yar Estuary before crossing to Freshwater village and continuing to the south coast at Freshwater Bay, nearly three miles. The northern half from Yarmouth to Freshwater Village was later opened as a continuation of the railway from Newport.

Southampton

Situated at the head of Southampton Water, on a peninsula between the rivers Test and Itchen, the port of Southampton has a history going back to Roman times, and still has its eleventh- century Bargate which influenced the design of its trams nine hundred years later. The London and South Western Railway took over the docks in 1892, and the Southern Railway built new docks on land reclaimed from the sea in the 1930's to service the Queen Mary and other ships crossing the Atlantic.

The Avenue is viewed from College Place as Southampton Corporation uncanopied open-top car No.55 bound for the Docks approaches the junction at College Place.
(J Welch & Sons, courtesy A.W. Brotchie

The Southampton Tramways Company introduced horse trams on 5 May 1879 under an Act of 1877. Routes eventually ran to Shirley, Portswood, and the Docks via Holy Rood. These were served by 31 open-top tramcars with knifeboard seating on the upper deck, a necessary feature to allow passage through the Bargate. Southampton Corporation purchased the Company's assets on 1 July 1898, but the horse trams ran for a further two years, followed by a temporary service some months later.

Shirley was the first route to be converted to electric traction, on 15 January 1900, with a formal opening ceremony on 22 January and the other routes followed five months later. Several extensions were built up to 1930, when the Swaythling and Bassett routes were linked via Burgess Road. The two main city termini were Royal Pier serving the Isle of Wight steamers and the Docks serving the LSWR Terminus station. Latterly service 1 linked both these termini with Swaythling and Bassett via High Street or St.Mary's, while service 4 linked Bitterne Park with the Docks, also via High Street. or St.Mary,s. Other services were 5 Shirley-Floating Bridge via High Street, 6 Docks-Millbrook, and 7 Northam-Shirley.

Although the Northam route was abandoned in 1936 and a trolleybus Act was obtained in 1937, the trams continued to serve the city until 31 December 1949, when the last route, to Shirley, was converted to motorbus operation.

Southampton was served by an interesting and varied fleet of over 100 four-wheel tramcars. All the early cars were open-top with knifeboard seating, and those built from 1923 onwards were enclosed with small wheels, low floors, and domed roofs, thus enabling them all to pass through the Bargate. Other cars included six ex-LCC Class B cars and ten English Electric balcony cars bought in 1918 and 1919. These latter could not pass beneath the Bargate, but by 1938 this had been by-passed on both sides.

A number of Southampton trams have survived. No.45 was purchased for £10 in 1948, and travelled some 1,200 miles before arriving at Crich Tramway Village, the home of the National Tramway Museum. Other cars being restored locally by 'The Tram 57 Project" include domed-roof car No.11, and knifeboards Nos.38 and 57.

Hythe Pier

A 1½ mile ferry operates across Southampton Water from the Town Quay to Hythe Pier, 2,100 feet long, upon which a tramway was built in July 1909. Initially two trucks were propelled by hand, but these were replaced by a new two-foot gauge tramway opened in July 1922 by then pier owners, the General Estates Co.Ltd. In 1992 ownership of both ferries and tramway but not the pier, passed to White Horse Ferries Ltd. The single train, Brush locomotive plus three Drewry bogie trailers, has current collection by a third-rail on the south-east side of the pier and provides a connection with each ferry sailing.

Under the Totton, Hythe & Fawley Light Railway Order of 1903 the Southern Railway opened the standard-gauge branch to Fawley on 20 July 1925. As it was easier to reach Hythe by ferry from Southampton the line was closed to passengers in the 1970's, but still serves the oil refinery at Fawley.

Lyndhurst

Eight miles west-south-west of Southampton or eight from Hythe, Lyndhurst in the New Forest had a population of 4,000 in 1901 when the Lyndhurst Electric Lighting & Traction Co. Ltd. was authorised to build 2½ miles of standard-gauge line from the town centre along the side of what is now the A35 road to Lyndhurst Road LSWR Station. Sadly the line was never built.

Bournemouth

In a sheltered pine valley between the ancient town of Christchurch on the river Avon and the port of Poole to the west, Bournemouth, thanks also to its fine sandy beach, developed rapidly as a seaside resort during the nineteenth century.

The proposal in 1898 by the BET to extend its Poole line through Bournemouth to Christchurch spurred the Bournemouth Corporation, initially opposed to tramways, into action, and the Bournemouth Corporation Tramways Act was obtained in 1901. So also was the BET Act, for a tramway from Bournemouth (Lansdowne) to Pokesdown, within Bournemouth Borough, and to Christchurch. The BET could only build their line within the Borough if Bournemouth failed to build theirs within two years. The Corporation however opened its tramway on 23 July 1902 from Lansdowne to Pokesdown, and it was extended to Christchurch on 17 October 1905 after Bournemouth had obtained a further Act in that year, and a through service was then introduced from Poole to Christchurch, the Poole system, with two routes, having been leased in 1905.. Other Corporation lines served Holderness Road, Charminster Road, and Moordown.

The centre of the system was The Square, and conduit tracks were initially laid for up to half a mile on the three routes approaching this area, but were replaced by standard overhead wires in 1911. The 'main line' service, Christchurch-Poole, was operated by open-top bogie cars, and the other routes by four-wheelers. Of the 17 ex-Poole and District trams serving the Upper Parkstone route, all except one, which went to Llandudno, were scrapped in 1922, when new bogie cars were purchased.

The trams operated profitably for over thirty years, but the last Poole service, via Upper Parkstone, was replaced by Hants and Dorset motor buses when the lease expired on 8 June 1935, The final Bournemouth tram, No.115, ran from Christchurch to The Square on 8 April 1936, trolleybuses taking over next day. Tram No.1, a luxury tram for private hire, survived for many years as a trolleybus passenger shelter at Iford. Ten bogie cars saw further service in Llandudno, of which No.85 has been preserved at the Museum of Electricity, Christchurch.

A busy scene in Christchurch Road, Boscombe, probably before the extension to Christchurch was opened on 5 October 1905. Single truck Milnes-built Bournemouth Corporation No.40 would terminate at Boscombe.
(LL commercial card,courtesy A.W. Brotchie.

There are three cliff lifts in Bournemouth: West Cliff, East Cliff, and Fisherman's Walk at Pokesdown. The first two were opened in 1908 and the last in 1935 to serve this growing residential area. They are all electrically operated, with a motor at the top station. The gauge is 5ft. 6in., with the rails on timber baulks concreted in to the cliff face.

Poole

Moving westwards from Bournemouth we reach the ancient port of Poole which developed at the head of a fine natural harbour sheltered by the Isle of Purbeck. The British Electric Traction Company (BET) saw the potential for a tramway to Bournemouth, and in 1899 obtained a Light Railway Order for a line from Poole Station via Upper Parkstone to Bournemouth County Gates, the Borough and County boundary. Built to the 3ft. 6in. gauge it was to be single-line with passing loops and operated by the Poole and District Electric Traction Company Limited. and opened on 6 April 1901. Proposals for extensions down to Poole Harbour and Canford Cliffs did not materialise, but the Lower Parkstone loop line was built by Poole Corporation and opened on 3 August 1906. Meanwhile Poole Corporation had purchased the company tramway on 15 June 1903 and for two years Bournemouth worked it for them by agreement. Then from June 1905 Poole leased it and the new 1906 line to Bournemouth Corporation for 30 years.

Swanage

Swanage, a market town on the Isle of Purbeck, nearly had a tramway connection to Bournemouth. This was an ambitious proposal in 1905 by the Branksome Park and Swanage Light Railway Company to build a 13¼ mile, 3ft. 6in. tramway from the town via Studland and Sandbanks to Branksome Park and County Gates in Bournemouth, with a branch from Sandbanks to Lower Parkstone. The line, which would have involved a climb from sea level to over 300 feet at Dean Hill, was not authorised. There would have been a transporter bridge over the entrance to Poole Harbour replacing Sandbanks ferry.

Built originally at Eastbourne by Modern Electric Tramways, No.8 is seen at Seaton on 13 April 1980 before rebuilding in 1992 with open cross bench seating.

(R.J.S.Wiseman.

Weymouth

The Borough of Weymouth, with ferry services to the Channel Islands, was until recently served by the one-mile Weymouth Harbour Tramway, opened on 1 July 1889, along the public roads down to the ferry terminal. The ferry, except for one daily service, was transferred to Poole in 1986 and the last trains to use the tramway were two enthusiasts specials in 1988. The town might have had a short one-mile 3ft. gauge horse-operated tramway from Southfield Road via Dorchester Road and along the Esplanade to St.Mary Street if the 1884 proposals of the Weymouth District Tramways Company had borne fruit.

Seaton

Seaton is now a popular seaside resort, which developed on the west side of the River Axe following the opening of the London & South Western Railway branch line from Seaton Junction. The branch closed on 7 March 1966 and, following the closure of the Eastbourne tramway on 14 September 1969, the track, poles and equipment were transferred to Seaton early in 1970, with the rolling stock following during that year.

The new track was laid to a gauge of 2ft.9in. and preparations began in 1970 using battery power and tram No.8, This ran from Riverside Depot as far as Bodsworth Bridge until 1971, when the battery service was extended to Colyford. Erection of the overhead line was completed to Colyford in 1973 and energised at 120 volts DC, and the new service began on 23 September. At Seaton, the tramway was extended from the former railway alignment to the car park in the town centre in 1975, where a new terminal building was opened in 1995. At the Colyford end the line was extended to Colyton and opened on 8 March 1980.

An interesting variety of trams is operated on the line and includes open-top double-deckers, single-deckers and a toastrack. The line follows the railway alignment along the west bank of the River Axe, and birdwatchers specials are run throughout the year. At Colyford there is a light-controlled level crossing over the main Lyme Regis - Exeter road (A3052). Trams operate daily during the summer from Easter to the end of October, and at weekends November to mid December and February to March, but these dates are subject to change.

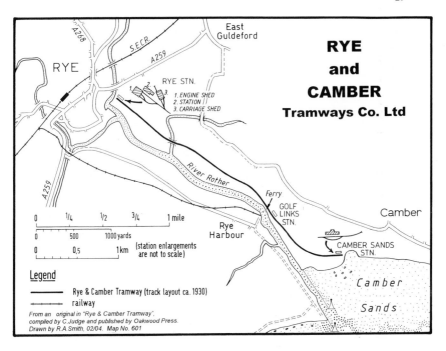

Rye & Camber train hauled by 0-4-2 tank "Victoria" leaving Camber Sands pulling two closed coaches plus two open wagons. These were originally used for transportation of ammunition during World War 1. They were converted into open carriages seating 20 passengers on transverse seats.

(Courtesy National Tramway Museum.

...and "The New" at Silverhill.

A busy scene at the junctions at Silverhill, Hastings. The trams on the left are working a Hollington-St.Helens Cemetery service via Bohemia and those on the right the circular service via Baldslow.

(Courtesy National Tramway Museum.

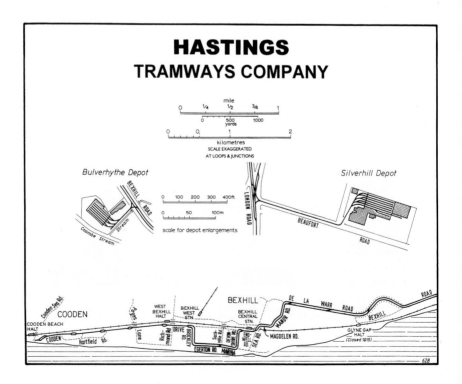

HASTINGS
TRAMWAYS COMPANY

The first trams arrived in July 1905 and caused much excitement. No.13 has arrived from the depot via Beaufort Road and is about to turn south into London road. Kilnhurst, an old house long demolished, was the original name for the Cooden Beach route. As this did not open until 28 July 1906 the picture may date from that time.
(Courtesy A.W. Brotchie.

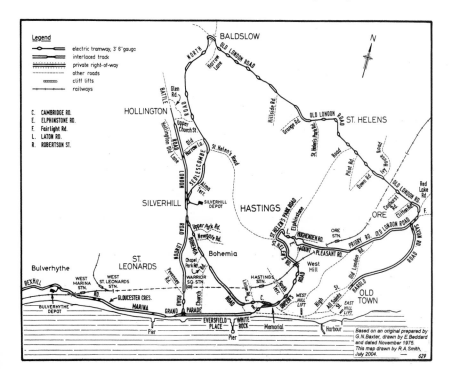

HASTINGS CONTRASTS

Conduit operation lasted on the Hastings Promenade from 12 January 1907 until 26 March 1914. In this view of No.60 the wire brush which checks that the stud is no longer live is visible at the back of the tram.

(Courtesy National Tramway Museum.

No.24, destination St.Helens, passes under St. Andrew's Arch in Queens Road, which still carries the railway line from Hastings to Ashford.

(Courtesy A.W.Brotchie.

THE HASTINGS CIRCULAR ROUTE

On a trial run in July 1905 No.2, having passed beyond the Congregational Church in Mount Pleasant Road, is approaching the sharp corner into Elphinstone Road.
(Commercial card, courtesy A.W.Brotchie.

No.30, on the circular service anti-clockwise via Ore, is at St.Helen's Cemetery, terminus for the trams going to Hollington
(J.O.Forster series, courtesy A.W.Brotchie.

This circular route was also very popular with visitors, and here we see No.13 in a sylvan setting before the motor car era.
(Courtesy National Tramway Museum.

34

The London Road track was single as it approached the sea at St. Leonards. The destination screen shows Silverhill while the position of the trolley arm seems to indicate that No.34 is about to reverse back up the hill.

(J.H.Price collection courtesy National Tramway Museum.

The electric locomotive and the electric passenger car at work on the Hellingly line soon after the opening.

(R.B.Parr, National Tramway Museum.

BRIGHTON TRAMCARS 1901-1932

Brighton's initial fleet of forty trams was built by Milnes in 1901-2. No.4, seen in original condition, was scrapped in 1924 and replaced by a new Class B car.
(National Tramway Museum

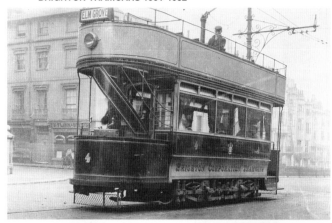

The first Class B car was built at Lewes Road in 1914, and the last, No.32, seen here in the depot entrance on 6 March 1938, in 1926.
(W.A.Camwell, National Tramway Museum.

In 1932 No.26(ii) was the last Class E car to be built at Lewes Road. It is seen here in original condition on the Queens Park Road route.
(H.B.Priestley, National Tramway Museum.

36

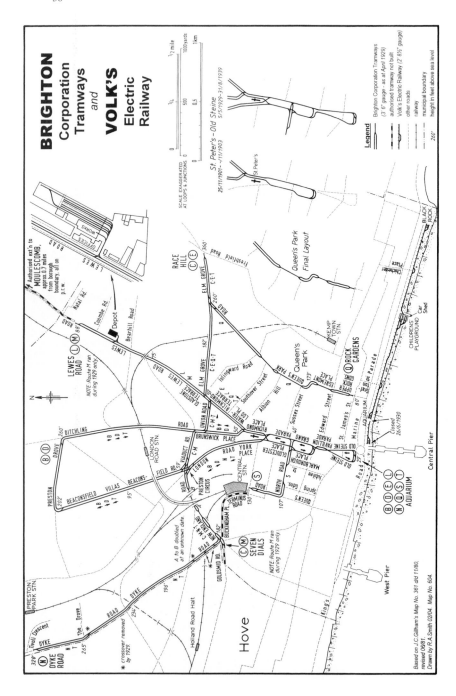

BRIGHTON TRAMCARS 1929-1933

No.69, also Class E, was built in 1929 and is seen in New England Road on service C from Seven Dials to Queen's Park.

(W.A.Camwell, National Tramway Museum.

Class F car No.58 was built at Lewes Road in 1933 and is seen at Dyke Road terminus. This was the only Brighton route not replaced by trolleybuses. A sign on the pole offers a 2d return fare.

(W.A.Camwell, National Tramway Museum.

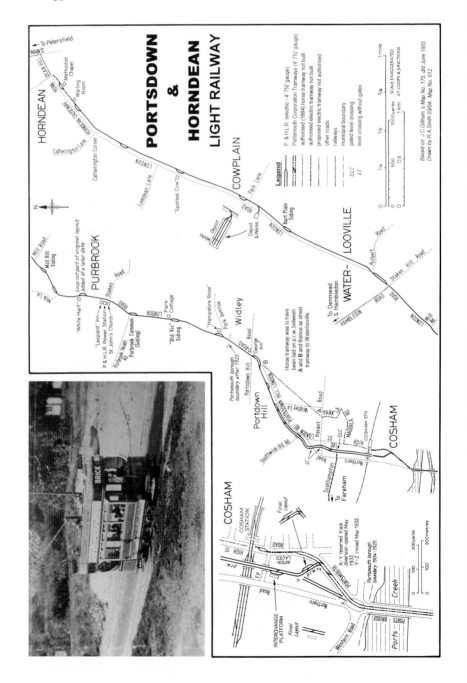

PORTSDOWN
&
HORNDEAN
LIGHT RAILWAY

HORNDEAN

To Petersfield
MAIN ST.
Methodist Chapel
Waiting Room
Catherington Corner
Catherington Lane
COWPLAIN
Lovedean Lane
"Spotted Cow"O
Park Lane
Hart Plain Siding
Depot & Works
WATER-LOOVILLE
Hulbert Road
Stakes Hill Road
PURBROOK
Mill Road
Mill Hill Siding
Loop not part of original layout added at a later date
Stakes Road
"White Hart" O
"Leopard" Inn
P & H.L.R. Power Station
St John's Church
Purbrook Heath Rd
Purbrook Common (Siding)
"Old Vic" Siding
Park Cottage
Widley
"Hampshire Rose"
Park Avenue
George Inn
To Denmead & Hambledon
HAMBLEDON ROAD
Portsmouth borough boundary after 1920
Portsdown Hill
Horse tramway was to have been laid on p.i.w. between A and B and thence as street tramway to Waterlooville
B
Widley La.
PARK A LA
Havant Road
MAGDALA RD
COSHAM STN
COSHAM
Southwick Hill Rd
Northern Road
Southampton Road
To Fareham

Legend

P. & H.L.R. (electric - 4' 7¾" gauge)
Portsmouth Corporation Tramways (4' 7¾" gauge)
authorised (1884) horse tramway not built
authorised electric tramway not built
proposed electric tramway not authorised
other roads
railways
municipal boundary
gated level crossing
GLC
LC level crossing without gates

1 mile
SCALE EXAGGERATED
AT LOOPS & JUNCTIONS
1000 yards
1 km

Based on J.C.Gillham 's Map No 175, dtd June 1955.
Drawn by R.A.Smith 03/04. Map No. 612

COSHAM
COSHAM STATION
HIGH ST
Final Layout
P.i.w.
INTER-LACED
F.P.
X-Y reserved track diversion opened May 1932.
Y-Z closed May 1932
Portsmouth borough boundary 1904–1920
Northern Road
Western Road
PORTS BRIDGE
Creek
Ports
INTERCHANGE PLATFORM
Final Layout
200 yards
200 metres

PORTSMOUTH - HORNDEAN INTERURBAN -1

Brush car No.16 at Canoe Lake, South Parade Pier, awaits departure to Horndean via Portsmouth tracks as far as Cosham. Note Corporation car No.44 behind.
(Dr.H.Nicol, National Tramway Museum.

No 14 (ii) ex No. 20 in the Fareham fleet is posed in Cowplain Depot yard.
(Dr. H. Nicol, National Tramway Museum.
Opposite:- Viewed from the top of Portsdown Hill No.3 is almost there!
(Courtesy P.Hewson.

PORTSMOUTH - HORNDEAN INTERURBAN -2

Beyond Cosham the line climbed Portsdown Hill, and No.16 is now descending on its way back to Portsmouth.

(Commercial card, courtesy National Tramway Museum.

At The George Inn the tram took to the main London Road. Here No.3 has followed the bendy road south from Waterlooville on its way towards Cosham

(Gurnell card courtesy A.W.Brotchie

It was sleeper track roadside reservation from Waterlooville to the terminus at Horndean, where No.2 waits to start the return journey.

(Lillywhite card, courtesy A.W.Brotchie)

41

PORTSMOUTH SCENES

A busy scene at Clarence Pier, Southsea, before the new loop layout was constructed in 1925. Ex-horse tram No.84 destined for Eastney is now at the Hampshire Museum at Basingstoke.

(Schwerdfeger card, courtesy National Tramway Museum.

The 'standard' Portsmouth tramcar was an open-top three-window Preston product built in 1900-01. Over thirty years old No. 14 is showing its age by 1932. An extra for Twyford Avenue is loading at South Parade Pier.

(M.J.O'Connor, National Tramway Museum.

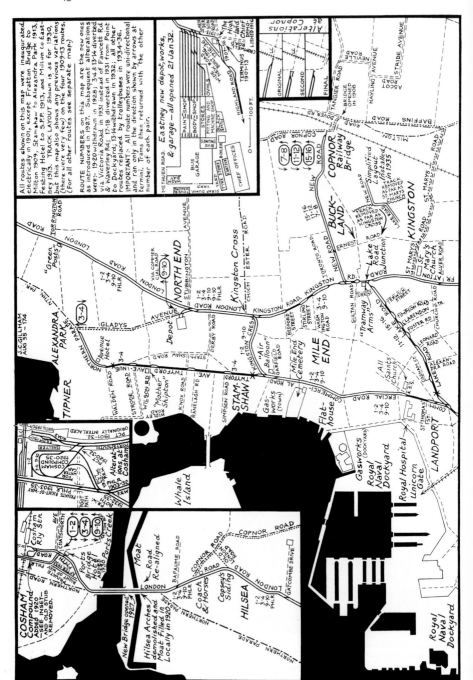

43

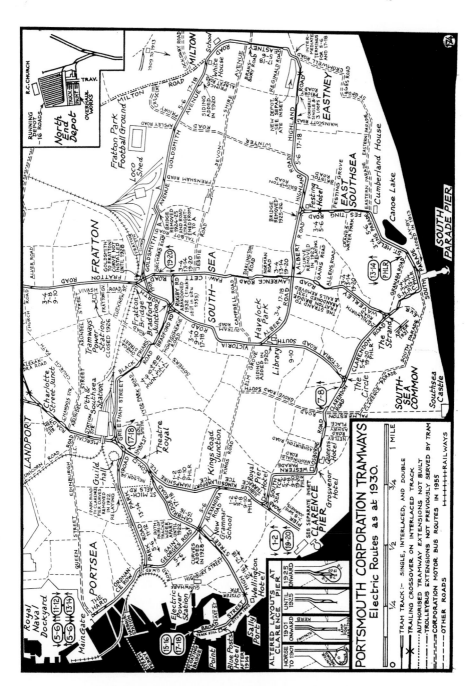

PORTSMOUTH CORPORATION TRAMWAYS
Electric Routes as at 1930.

Nos.85-100 were delivered from Preston in 1906-07. No.100 at South Parade Pier is on a short working to Milton in 1932.
(M.J.O'Connor, National Tramway Museum.

Twelve enclosed trams, again from Preston, followed in 1920 and No.106 is at South Parade Pier.
(Dr.H.A.Whitcombe Science Museum, Science and Society Picture Library.

Ben Hall, the new general manager, came from Halifax in 1926 and immediately improved much of the rolling stock. In 1930 No.1 was built to his design. Seen at the Guildhall, it ended its days at Sunderland.
(M.J.O'Connor, National Tramway Museum.

GOSPORT - FAREHAM INTERURBAN -1

Three views of the corner of West Street and Portland Street in Fareham.

Above:- No.10 is heading west down West Street towards the station terminus while middle, No.8 is waiting to turn into Portland Street from West Street and below No.4 is about to turn into West Street with Fareham Town Hall behind the tram.

(two National Tramway Museum, middle P.Hewson.

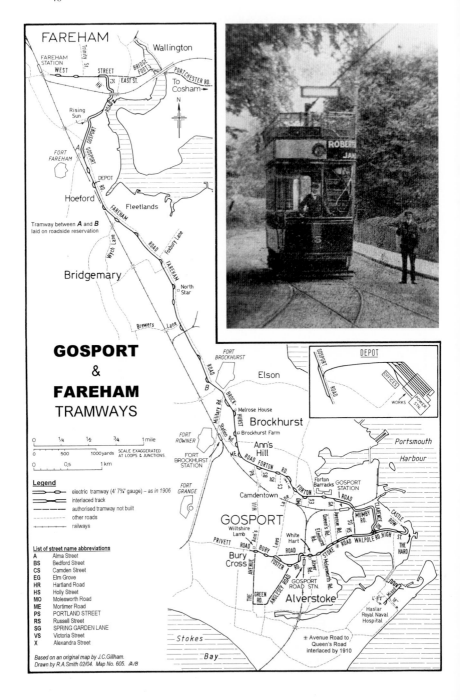

FAREHAM

Wallington

FAREHAM
STATION
WEST

STREET

EAST ST.

BRIDGE
FOOT

Trinity St.

HR

X

PORTCHESTER RD.
To
Cosham

N

Rising
Sun

FORT
FAREHAM

GOSPORT ROAD

A

DEPOT

Hoeford

FAREHAM RD.

Fleetlands

Tramway between *A* and *B*
laid on roadside reservation

Wych Lane

FAREHAM ROAD

Foxbury Lane

Bridgemary

North
Star

Brewers Lane

GOSPORT
&
FAREHAM
TRAMWAYS

FORT
BROCKHURST

Elson

ROAD

B

BROCKHURST

Melrose House

Brockhurst Farm

FORT
ROWNER

Station Rd.

Brockhurst

Portsmouth

Harbour

Legend

electric tramway (4' 7¾" gauge) – as in 1906
interlaced track
authorised tramway not built
other roads
railways

FORT
BROCKHURST
STATION

Military Rd.

Ann's
Hill

ME ROAD

FORTON

FORTON RD.

BS

CS

Forton
Barracks

GOSPORT
STATION

93

ROAD

Camdentown

La Rue

MO

List of street name abbreviations

A	Alma Street
BS	Bedford Street
CS	Camden Street
EG	Elm Grove
HR	Hartland Road
HS	Holly Street
MO	Molesworth Road
ME	Mortimer Road
PS	PORTLAND STREET
RS	Russell Street
SG	SPRING GARDEN LANE
VS	Victoria Street
X	Alexandra Street

Based on an original map by J.C.Gillham.
Drawn by R.A.Smith 02/04. Map No. 605. IA/B

FORT
GRANGE

GOSPORT

Wiltshire
Lamb

PRIVETT

ROAD

Ann's

BURY

White
Hart

Queen's Rd.

Elmhurst Rd.

Avenue Rd.

STOKE ROAD

Alver Rd.

Molesworth Rd.

MUMBY
RD.

SG

HS

WALPOLE RD.

CLARENCE

CASTLE

ROW

HIGH

ST.

THE
HARD

Bury
Cross

THE AVENUE

THE
GREEN
RD.

FOSTER

ROAD

ANGLESEY ROAD

GOSPORT
ROAD STN.

Alverstoke

‡ Avenue Road to
Queen's Road
interlaced by 1910

4'8½" Mixed Ga.

Haslar
Royal Naval
Hospital

Stokes

Bay

SCALE
0   ¼   ½   ¾   1 mile
0   500   1000 yards   SCALE EXAGGERATED
                        AT LOOPS & JUNCTIONS.
0   0,5   1 km

DEPOT

GOSPORT ROAD

OFFICES

WORKS

POWER
STN.

47

GOSPORT - FAREHAM INTERURBAN - 2

The tramway was on roadside reservation south from F a r e h a m Harbour, and, above, No.6 is passing the Hoeford Inn just south of the depot. It was then through open country to B r o c k h u r s t, where No.3 is seen, middle, by the Wheatsheaf. Finally we reach Gosport High Street where No.11 displays Fareham on its d e s t i n a t i o n screen.

(National Tramway Museum, (top). others, A.W.Brotchie.

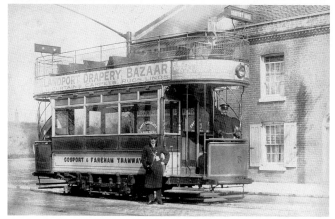

Opposite: The Bury Cross route terminated at Privett Road, where this picture of No.5 was posed.

(P.Hewson.

48

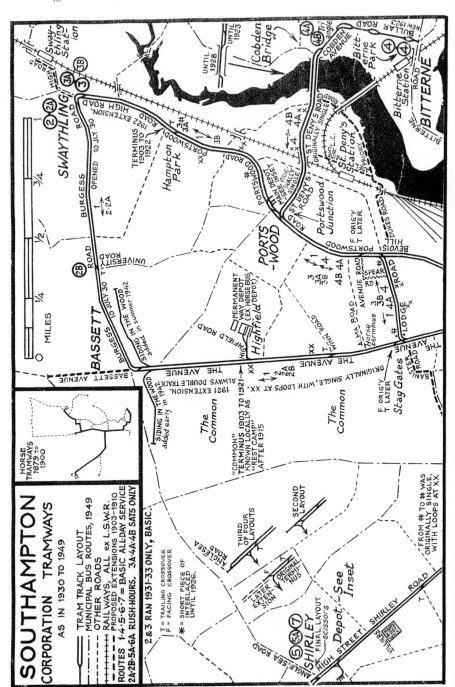

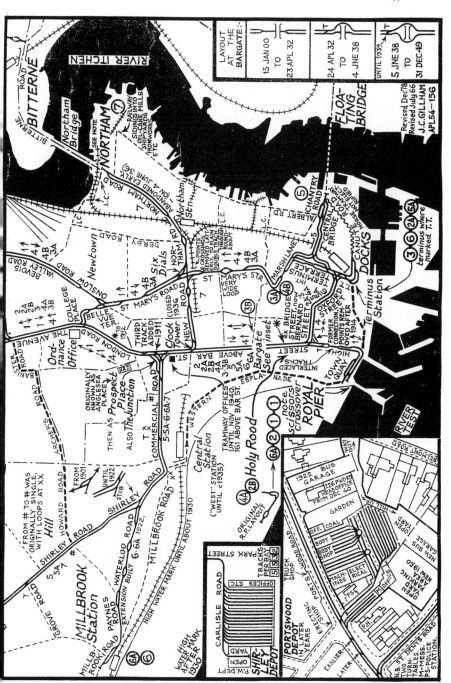

SOUTHAMPTON CONTRASTS

Southampton Tramway Company Starbuck-built horse tram No. 19, dating from the 1880's, is probably in Shirley.

(Courtesy National Tramway Museum.

In Shirley Road at the junction with Waterloo Road No.20 has followed No.16 past the remnants of the points leading to Milbrook on the last day of operation, 31 December 1949.

(J.H.Meredith.

SOUTHAMPTON BARGATE

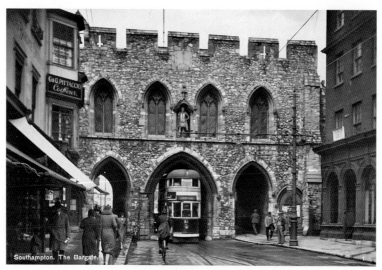

The Bargate always influenced the design of Southampton's trams, initially knifeboard seats on the open upper-deck and latterly domed-roof trams. Above:- Uncanopied Milnes car No.18 is heading south while, below, No.31, one of the first domed-roof cars, is heading north circa. 1930. The Bargate was by-passed in two stages. A new road on the east side for southbound traffic was opened on 24th April 1932 and later on the west side for northbound traffic on 5th June 1938.

(Courtesy National Tramway Museum and A.W.Brotchie.)

SOUTHAMPTON TRAMCARS 1914 - 1919

No.72, an open top canopied car with knifeboard seats, was built in 1914. It is seen here at Shirley.
(National Tramway Museum.

No.78, an ex-LCC B Class car, bought in 1918, with upper-deck roof and seats removed, is seen Below Bar in 1932.
(M.J.O'Connor, National Tramway Museum.

English Electric balcony car No.84, built in 1919, outside Shirley Depot, 23 September 1942.
(M.J.O'Connor, National Tramway Museum.

SOUTHAMPTON DOMED-ROOF CARS

No.16(iii) was one of the first of those built in 1923-29 at Portswood. Seen here, well loaded, in Shirley Road on 23 October 1948.

(J.H.Meredith.

On 19 April 1949 No.99 was photographed in Commercial Road on 18 April 1949

(R.J.S.Wiseman.

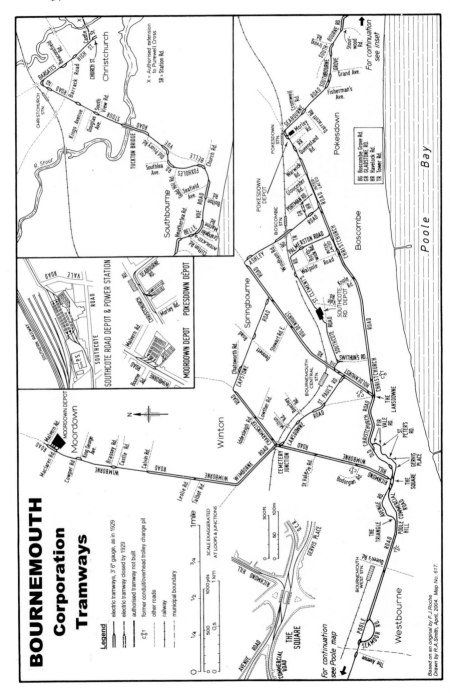

BOURNEMOUTH Corporation Tramways

Legend

electric tramways, 3'6" gauge, as in 1929
electric tramway closed by 1929
authorised tramway not built
c&t former conduit/overhead trolley change pit
other roads
railway
municipal boundary

SCALE EXAGGERATED AT LOOPS & JUNCTIONS

1000 yds
1 km

X = Authorised extension to Purewell Cross
SR = Station Rd.

Based on an original by F.J Roche
Drawn by R.A.Smith, April, 2004. Map No. 617.

Bg Boscombe Grove Rd.
GR GLADSTONE RD.
HR Havelock Rd.
TR Tower Rd.

BOURNEMOUTH TO CHRISTCHURCH

The Square was the hub of the Bournemouth system. This view looking east sees five tramcars after removal of the conduit track in 1913 and before the building of the passenger shelter in 1925.

(Commercial card, courtesy A.W.Brotchie.

In order for trams to reach Christchurch the wooden toll bridge over the river Stour had to be replaced by the stronger structure seen here. The extension was opened on 17 October 1905.

(G.W.Neeve card, courtesy National Tramway Museum.

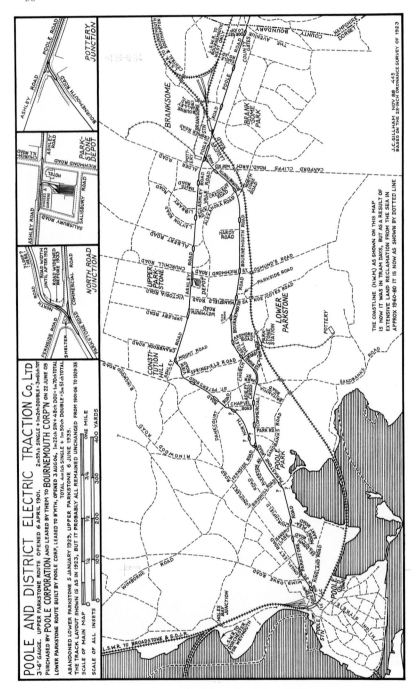

TRAMS IN POOLE

Bournemouth No.30 on the long length of single track in Bournemouth Road, Lower Parkstone.

(Commercial card, courtesy A.W.Brotchie.

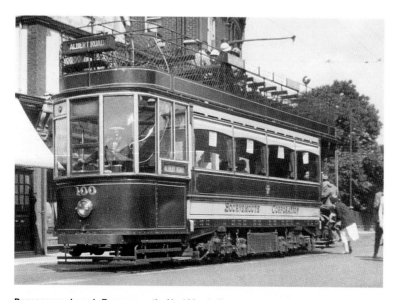

Passengers board Bournemouth No.100 at the eastern end of Seamoor Road, Westbourne. Albert Road was the destination used for the depot at Upper Parkstone.

(M.J.O'Connor, National Tramway Museum.

CONTRASTING SCENES

The long ten mile through route from Poole Station ended 90 minutes later in Church Street, Christchurch, in sight of the Priory Church.

(LL Series, courtesy A.W.Brotchie.

Snow is rare in Bournemouth and any available car appears to have been used during the winter of 1908 or 1909 in Boscombe.

(G.H. Stanford, 'Up-to-date Series', courtesy A.W.Brotchie.

No.6, as rebuilt in 1990 with crossbench seating throughout the lower section, is seen at Colyton.
(David Voice.

No.12, as rebuilt in 1999 with Feltham style driving cabins. is also at Colyton.
(David Voice.

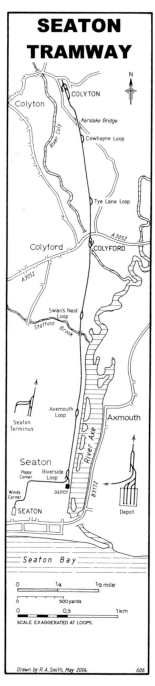

SEATON TRAMWAY

N

COLYTON

Colyton

Kerslake Bridge

Cowhayne Loop

Tye Lane Loop

A3052

Colyford   COLYFORD

A3052

Swan's Nest Loop

Stafford Brook

Axmouth Loop

Axmouth

Seaton Terminus

River Axe

Seaton

Poppy Corner   Riverside Loop

Windy Corner   DEPOT

B3172

SEATON

Depot

Seaton Bay

0   ¼   ½ mile

0   500 yards

0   0.5   1 km

SCALE EXAGGERATED AT LOOPS.

Drawn by R.A.Smith, May 2004   606

HYTHE PIER TRAMWAY

These two views of the Hythe Pier Tramway, taken in April 1953 show, above, the Hythe terminus and, below, Pier terminus in April 1953.

(M.G.C.W. Wheeler.

The half-mile length of the pier can be seen in this photograph of the Brush locomotive and three Drewery trailers. 23 July 1983.

(J.C.Gillham.

CLIFF LIFTS AT BOURNEMOUTH AND HASTINGS

The Fisherman's Walk lift at Bournemouth was opened in 1935.

(David Voice.

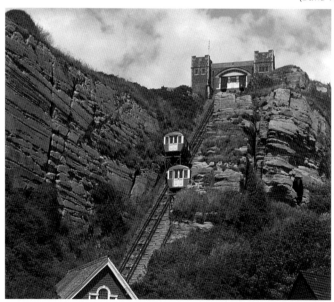

The East Hill lift at Hastings, in a cutting in the cliff face, dates back to 1903. Closed in 1973 it was re-opened with new cars in 1976.

(David Voice.

Tramcar Fleet Lists

All cars were four-wheel double-deck unless otherwise stated.

Seating figures shown thus: 22/34 are for lower and upper decks respectively.

The opening dates shown are the first day of regular public service.

The closing dates shown are the last full day of public service.

Bournemouth Corporation Tramways

16.11 miles, 3ft. 6in. gauge, opened 23 July 1902, closed 8 April 1936. Livery chocolate and primrose yellow. The trams except in Poole were replaced by trolleybuses which ran from 13 May 1933 until 30 April 1969.

Car Numbers	Type (as built)	Year Built	Builder	Seats	Truck(s)	Motors	Controllers
1 (a)	Single-deck	1902	Milnes	30	Brill 22E MxT bogies	Westinghouse 49B 2 x 30hp	Westinghouse 90
2- 20	Open top	1902	Milnes	30/32	Brill 22E MxT bogies	Westinghouse 49B 2 x 30hp	Westinghouse 90
21- 48	Open top	1902	Milnes	20/22	Peckham Cantilever	Westinghouse 49B 2 x 30hp	Westinghouse 90
49- 54 (b)	Open top	1904	Milnes	30/32	Brill 22E MxT bogies	Westinghouse 49B 2 x 30hp	Westinghouse 90
55- 58 (c)	Open top	Acquired 1905	Milnes	22/26	Brill 21E	BTH GE58-6T 2 x 28 hp	BTH B18
59-65 (d)	Open top uncanopied	Acquired 1905	ER&TCW	22/26	Brill 21E	BTH GE58-6T 2 x 28 hp	DK
66-71 (e)	Open top	Acquired 1905	Brush	22/26	Brush A	BTH GE58-6T 2 x 28 hp	Brush
72-81 (f)	Open top	1907	Brush	30/32	Brill 22E MxT bogies	Westinghouse 200 2 x 35hp	Westinghouse
82 (f)	Open top	Acquired 1905	Brush	22/26	Brush A	BTH GE58-6T 2 x 28hp	Brush
83-92 (g)	open top	1914	UEC	30/32	Brill 22E MxT bogies	Westinghouse W226 2 x 35/40hp	Westinghouse T1C
93-112 (h)	open top	1921	Brush	30/38	Brill 22E MxT bogies	BTH GE249 2 x 37hp	BTH B49CC
113-132 (i)	open top	1924-6	Brush	30/38	Brill 22E MxT bogies	MV 104Y 2 x 40 hp	MV T1C
B	Van	1903	Milnes	-	Peckham Cantilever	Westinghouse 49B 2 x 30hp	Westinghouse 90M

Notes

Nos.1-54, 72-81 were fitted for conduit operation.

(a) Special tram for private hire with luxury wicker chairs. Converted for service use in 1920.

(b) Three cars fitted 37hp BTH GE249A motors in 1921. Seating later 30/36.

(c) Ex-Poole Nos.1-4, built 1901, No.55 converted to a railgrinder in 1921. Sold to the Llandudno & Colwyn Bay Electric Tramway and renumbered 23A.

(d) Ex-Poole Nos.5-11, built 1901. Extended canopies fitted by Bournemouth.

(e) Ex-Poole Nos.12-17, built 1901-2.

(f) No.72 was renumbered 71 following an accident in 1908 and ex-Poole No.71 was renumbered 82. No.74 fitted 30hp Westinghouse B49 motors, c1922.

(g) Later vestibuled and seating became 30/36. No.89 fitted 37hp BTH GE249A motors in 1921. No.85 sold to Llandudno, renumbered 6 and now preserved at Bournemouth

(h) Vestibuled when built. Nos.95,103,108,112 sold to Llandudno; Nos.11,10,9,13 respectively. Body of No. 106 used in building Seaton 16.

(i) Vestibuled when built. Nos.114-6,121,128 sold to Llandudno; Nos. 15,7,8,14,12 respectively. No.7 being rebuilt at Llandudno. (2002) On closure the MV 104Y motors were sold to Liverpool Corporation. All cars sold to Llandudno, except No.85, L&CBER 6, had BTH GE 249A motors in Llandudno initially. Llandudno 12 fitted BTH B49 CC controllers ex-Bournemouth 98.

Hellingly Hospital

1.15 miles, 4ft. 8½ in. gauge, opened 20 July 1903, closed 25 March 1959, passengers in 1931. Electric locomotive by R. Blackwell and electric tramcar by Brush.

Brighton Corporation Tramways

9.48 miles, 3ft. 6in. gauge, opened 25 November 1901, closed 31 August 1939. Livery deep chocolate and primrose yellow; from c1930 brick red and cream. The trams were replaced by trolleybuses which operated from 1 May 1939 to 30 June 1961.

Car Numbers	Type (as built)	Year Built	Builder	Seats	Truck(s)	Motors	Controllers
1-30 (a)	Open top	1901	Milnes	26/26	Peckham Pendulum	Westinghouse 2 x 30hp	Westinghouse
31-40 (b)	Open top	1902	Milnes	26/26	Brush A	E&H 2 x 30hp	Westinghouse
41-50 (c)	Open top	1904-5	UEC	26/26	Brill 21E	DK 6A 2 x 35hp	DK DB1 Form E
51-53 (d)	Open top	1914	BCT	26/28	Brill 21E	DK 13A 2 x 40hp	DK DB1 Form K3
54-63 (e)	Open top	1919-22	BCT	26/26	Brill 21E	DK 30B 2 x 40hp	DK DB1 Form K3
43 cars (f)	Open top	1917-26	BCT	26/26	Brill 21E	DK 30B 2 x 40hp	DK DB1 Form K3B
8 cars (g)	Open top	1926-8	BCT	26/26	Brill 21E	DK 30B 2 x 40hp	DK DB1 Form K3B
64-67 (h)	Open top	1928	BCT	26/26	Brill 21E	DK 30B 2 x 40hp	DK DB1 Form K3B
68-80 (i)	Open top	1929-31	BCT	26/26	Brill 21E	DK 105/1c 2 x 50hp	DK DB1 Form K3E
4 cars (j)	Open top	1932	BCT	26/26	Brill 21E	DK 30B 2 x 40hp	DK DB1 Form K3B
31 cars (k)	Open top	1933-7	BCT	26/26	Brill 21E	DK 30B 2 x 40hp	DK DB1 K3B
- (l)	Van	1910	?	-	Brill 21E	Peckham Pendulum	DK ?

Notes

(a) Class A. Bodies rebuilt 1908-13. Trucks replaced by Brill 21E from 1908 to 1913. Nos.23,28 fitted 40hp DK 30B motors intended for Nos.54-55.

(b) Class A. Nos.33,36,40 fitted Brill 21E trucks and DK 30B motors by 1920.

(c) Class A. Nos.41,43,46-50, and possibly all, used as trailers during the 1914-18 war. When re-equipped all fitted 40hp DK 30B motors.

(d) Class B. No.53 had 2? standard 26/26 seating.

(e) Class B. Nos.54-55 were fitted with Westinghouse motors initially.

(f) Class B. 43 replacement cars numbered 1-12(ii),14-21(ii),23-33(ii), 36(ii),38-39(ii),41-44(ii),46-50(ii).

(g) Class C. 8 replacement cars numbered 10(iii),13(ii),22(ii),34-35(ii),37(ii),40(ii),45(ii). These, and all subsequent cars were vestibuled.

(h) Class D.

(i) Class E.

(j) Class E. Four replacement cars numbered 1(iii),7(iii),17(iii),26(iii).

(k) Class F. 31 replacement cars numbered 2(iii),9(iii),11(iii),14-15(iii), 20-21(iii),23-25(iii),27(iii),30(iii), 41-43(iii),46(iii),48-50(iii), 51-60(ii), 63(ii),74(ii). Simpler maroon and cream livery.
The 35 cars above retained their original trucks and 40hp DK30B motors except No.75(ii) DK 105/1c. It also had 26" wheels as in Class E. All others had 30"-34" wheels. No.74(ii) was unique in having latest style body when rebodied in 1936 after overturning.

(l) Obtained initially as a snowplough, adapted later as a snowplough and general breakdown vehicle.

The Brighton and Rottingdean Seashore Electric Tramway

2.92 miles, two 2ft. 8 in. gauge tracks with 18ft. between the outer rails. Ceremonial opening Saturday 28 November 1896, public opening Monday 30 November 1896, closed 21 February 1901. One car supported on four legs 23 feet long was built by the Gloucester Railway Carriage & Wagon Company Ltd.

The Brighton District Tramway Company

4.64 miles initially, then 4.15 miles, 3ft. 6in. gauge, opened 3 July 1884, steam and horse traction. In liquidation in 1888 and succeeded by a new company, The Brighton and District Tramway Company Ltd., horse traction only and in liquidation by May 1889.

Engines:- Nos.1,2, Wilkinson,1884, sold to Wigan & District Tramways Co. in 1893, their Nos.5,6. No.3(?), Aveling and Porter, 1886. Livery dark brown. Trailers:-Nos.1,2, double-deck, Falcon, 1884.seating 64. Horse cars:-Nos.1-3, 1886, single-deck saloons seating 10 inside and five on each platform. Nos.4-10, 1886, double-deck. One car, probably No.10, was used experimentally for accumulator operation on 29 July 1887. Livery light brown.

Royal Naval Hospital Haslar. This view shows the standard gauge track leading direct to the hospital, and the narrow gauge line to the stores at Fort Monckton.

(Courtesy M. Petch.

Volks Railway, Brighton

1.29 miles, 2ft.8½ in. gauge, opened 4 August 1883 on 2ft. gauge, closed 13 January 1884; re-opened 4 April 1884 initially on 2ft.8 in. gauge, closed 2 July 1940. Re-opened 15 May 1948. Livery mahogany stain and varnish, brown and yellow from 1962. The line was purchased by Brighton Corporation from 1 April 1939, leased back to Volk for one year, and operation taken over by the Corporation from 1 April 1940.

Car numbers	Type (as built)	Year built	Builder	Seating as built	Motor	Notes
-	Saloon	1883	Volk	24	Volk 1 x 1 hp	(a) Scrapped 1884
1 - 2	Saloon	1884	Volk	30	Siemens 1 x 6hp	Scrapped 1948 (b)
3 - 4	Semi-open	1892	Volk	30?	Siemens? 1 x 7hp	(c)
5	Saloon	1897	Volk	30?	Siemens	(d) Scrapped 1933,
6 - 8	Semi-open	1901	Volk	32	CEB 1 x 8hp	(e) No.8 now 5(iii),
9	Cross-bench	1910	Volk	40	?	Now No.2(ii),
10	Cross-bench	1927	?	40	?	Renumbered 1(ii)
5(ii)	Saloon	1930	Kelsey	24	?	Scrapped 1948
8(ii) 9(ii)	Cross-bench	Bought 1949	Falcon	40	2 x 120v	(f)

Notes

The original cars have all been rebuilt since 1960. Controllers were originally of the open stud type on the canopy above the driver's head; these were replaced in 1963 by a simple ratchet type.

(a) 2ft. 0in. gauge.

(b) No.1 renumbered 5 in 1897. (Note d).

(c) Worm gear assembly by Greenwood & Batley of Leeds, to Anthony Reckenzaum designs. Re-equipped with conventional 8hp motors c1901, rebuilt over the years and now seating 40 on cross benches.

(d) Details not known, used original motor of 1884, chain and belt drive. Later renumbered 1(ii).

(e) Rebuilt over the years and now seating 40.

(f) Purchased 1948 via a dealer; ex-Southend Pier. Entered service in 1950 and 1953 respectively.

The Brighton and Shoreham Tramways Company Ltd.

4.15 miles, 3ft.6in. gauge, horse tracion, re-opened the line in November 1889 with three single-deck and one other, possibly No.10, later renumbered 4(ii). Nos.5-9(ii), 1891, double-deck; Nos.10(ii),11,12, 1900, double-deck later cut down to single-deck. Livery yellow. Closed 6 June 1913.

Gosport Street Tramways Company

2.62 miles, 3ft. 0in. gauge. Horse traction. Opened 17 July 1882, closed early in 1905 for reconstruction and electrificaion.

Rolling stock:- 8 single-deck cars plus a few double-deck with knifeboard seats.

Gosport and Fareham Tramwway

Owned by the Portsmouth Street Tramways Company.

7.75 miles, 4ft. 7¾ in.gauge, opened 24 January 1906, closed 31 December 1929. Livery emerald green and cream; during the 1914-18 war some cars were painted in a grey and white livery.

Car Numbers	Type (as built)	Year Built	Builder	Seats	Truck(s)	Motors	Controllers
1 - 12	Open top	1905	Brush	22/33	Brush 21E	?	?
13 - 22	Open top	1906	Milnes Voss	22/33	M&G 21EM	?	?

On closure Nos.2,8,10,14,20-22 were transferred to the Portsdown and Horndean Light Railway and another twelve were transferred to the associated Great Grimsby Street Tramways Company and renumbered 1 - 3 and 22 - 30..

The Haslar Tramway

400 yards, 4ft.8½ in. gauge, to Hospital entrance plus 1.50 miles 18 inch gauge to Fort Monckton for conveying stores.. Opened circa 1877, closed sometime after 1918.

One single-deck tramcar built by the Midland Railway Carriage and Wagon Co.,Ltd.

Hastings and District Electric Tramways Company Ltd

19.34 miles, 3ft. 6in. gauge, opened 31 July 1905, closed 15 May 1929. Livery maroon and cream. The trams were replaced by trolleybuses which ran from 1 April 1928 to 31 May 1959.

Car Numbers	Type (as built)	Year Built	Builder	Seats	Truck(s)	Motors	Controllers
1 - 30 a)	Open top	1905	ER& TCW	20/22	Brill 21E	DK 6A 2 x 35hp	DK DB1 Form E
31 - 40	Open top	1905	ER& TCW	20/22	Brill 21E	DK 6A 2 x 35hp	DK DB1 Form E
41 - 60 (b)	Open top	1906	UEC	20/22	Brill 21E	DK 6A 2 x 35hp	DK DB1 Form E
61 - 65	Open top	1907	UEC	20/22	Brill 21E	DK 6A 2 x 35hp	DK DB1 Form E (G?)

Notes

Stud contact operation was used along the sea front from 12 January 1907 until 26 March 1914; replaced by petrol-electric until March 1921. 40 40hp EE DK 30/1H motors and EE DK K33B controllers were bought in 1925 and fitted to 20 cars, numbers not known, for use on hilly routes.

(a) Nos. 2 and 3 were used as required as works cars.

(b) These cars were equipped with Dolter stud equipment from new; all or most of these cars were equipped with Tilling-Stevens petrol-electric motors from 1914 to 1921.

Hythe Pier Tramway

2,100 feet, 0.39 miles, 2ft.0in. gauge, opened 31 July 1909, hand propelled, electric third-rail collection from July 1922. Still open today. Livery originally green, later with window frames cream. From 1963 main panels 'a light shade of Royal blue with white window frames, from 1996 main panels red.

Two Brush battery locomotives from Ministry of Munitions, Avonmouth,, built 1917, converted to third-rail traction, and four bogie trailers by Drewry.   2 Driving seating 16-18, 2 ordinary seating 18-20.

Tramcars Preserved

In addition to those noted in the text the following tramcar bodies have been rescued and await restoration or are being restored:- Bournemouth 13,21,60(Poole 6),71,113. Brighton 53, Hastings 45, 56 and Portsdown and Horndean 5, 13. The lower saloon, unrestored, of Bournemouth 86 is at Llandudno.

Portsdown and Horndean Tramway

Owned by Hampshire Light Railways (Electric) Company Ltd.

6.00 miles, 4ft. 7¾ in. gauge, opened 2 March 1903, from 19 April 1927 operated over 5.43 miles of Portsmouth Corporation track, closed 9 January 1935. Livery emerald green and cream.

Car Numbers	Type (as built)	Year Built	Builder	Seats	Truck(s)	Motors	Controllers
1 - 14	Open top	1903	BEC	21/33	BEC SB 60	Westinghouse	Westinghouse
15 - 16	Open top	1905	Brush	21/33	Brill 21E	Westinghouse	Westinghouse
17 (a)	Single-deck Tram coach	1922	GGTC	40	Brill 21E	?	?
5 cars (b)	Open top	1905	Brush	22/33	BEC SB60	?	?
2 cars (c)	Open top	1906	Milnes	22/33	M&G 21EM	?	?

Notes

(a) Built at Grimsby by the Great Grimsby Tramways Company, an associated Provincial company. Transferred in 1925.

(b) Nos.2,10,14,20 transferred from the Gosport and Fareham Tramway in 1930. Fitted with SB60 trucks and renumbered 2,17,10,14 respectively. Also No.8, its Brush 21E type truck replaced by 21EM type.

(c) Nos.21,22 also transferred from the Gosport and Fareham in 1930.

Landport and Southsea Tramways Company

2.15 miles, 4ft. 7¾ in. gauge, horse traction, opened 15 May 1865. Single-deck cars.

Portsmouth Street Tramways Company Ltd.

7.18 miles, 4ft. 7¾ in.gauge, opened 11 September 1874, horse traction. Eight single-deck cars, four yellow, four green, initially.

General Tramways Company of Portsmouth Ltd.

2.78 miles, 4ft. 7¾ in. gauge, opened 18 March 1878, horse traction. Single-deck cars.

The above three companies, were all under the control of the Provincial Tramways Company and were amalgamated under the Portsmouth Street Tramways Company in August 1883. Maximum fleet 65 trams on 12 miles of route. Purchased by Portsmouth Corporation 1 January 1901.

Portsmouth (Borough),Kingston,Fratton and Southsea Tramways Company.

3.58 miles, 4ft. 7¾ in. gauge, opened 26 November 1885, horse traction. Sold to the Provincial company in April or May 1892.

Portsmouth Corporation Tramways

17.70 miles, 4ft. 7¾ in. gauge, opened 24 September 1901, closed 10 November 1936. Livery crimson lake and cream. The trams were replaced by trolleybuses which operated from 4 August 1934 to 27 July 1963.

Car Numbers	Type (as built)	Year Built	Builder	Seats	Truck(s)	Motors	Controllers
1- 80 (a)	Open top	1900-1	ER&TCW	22/33	Brill 21E	DK 25A 2 x 25hp	DK DB1 Form B
81- 84 (b)	Open top	1880	Milnes	20/26	Brill 21E	DK 25A 2 x 25hp	DK DE1 Form B
85-100	Open top	1906-7	UEC	22/32	Brill 21E	DK 25A 2 x 25hp	DK DB1 Form E
101	Water car	1904	PCT	-	Brill 21E	DK 25A 2 x 25hp	DK DB1 Form E
102-103 (c)	Water car	1919	PCT	-	Brill 21E	DK 25A 2 x 25hp	DK DB1 Form K4
104 (d)	Single-deck toastrack	Bought 1919	SCT	42	Brill 21E	Westinghouse 2 x 25hp	Westinghouse 5915
105-116	Enclosed	1920	EE	22/36	EE 21E	DK 20A 2 x 40hp	DK DB1 Form K3
1 (e)	Enclosed Domed roof	1930	PCT	23/35	Peckham Cantilever	EE DK 121P 2 x 50hp	DK DB1 Form K33E

Notes

(a) No.80 was fitted with an experimental top cover from 1904 to 1907. Nos.10-12,17,24,29,36,40,43,48,49,51,55-57,64,73,80,99 rebuilt 1929-1935. Nos.10,11 vestibuled,.No.6 had MV controllers for a time.

(b) Horse tramcars purchased in 1896 from the North Metropolitan Tramways Co.Ltd., London. rebuilt in 1903.. No.84, used as a railgrinder until 1919 and is now preserved at the Hampshire County Council Museum at Basingstoke with DK DE1 controllers.

(c) No.103 was also used as a rail grinder.

(d) Ex-Southampton 2(ii). Fitted with a canopy,1930, then a boat body i933.

(e) Sold to Sunderland Corporation, renumbered 52(ii) and later 45(ii).

In 1919 Portsmouth Corporation bought the 'touring car' from Southampton. Numbered 104 it is seen in the North End Depot.

(Courtesy National Tramway Museum.

Poole and District Tramways Company Ltd

5.84 miles, 3ft. 6in. gauge, opened 6 April 1901, purchased by Poole Corporation on 15 June 1903 who leased to Bournemouth Corporation from June 1905. Closed 7 June 1935. Livery Cambridge blue and white.

Car Numbers	Type (as built)	Year Built	Builder	Seats	Truck(s)	Motors	Controllers
1 - 4	Open top	1901	Milnes	22/26	Brill 21E	BTH GE58-6T 2 x 28hp	BTH B18
5 - 11	Open top uncanopied	1901	ER&TCW	22/26	Brill 21E	BTH GE58-6T 2 x 28hp	DK
12 - 17	Open top	1901-2	Brush	22/26	Brush A	BTH GE58-6T 2 x 28hp	Brush

All these cars passed to Bournemouth Corporation in 1905 and were numbered 55-58, 59-65 and 66-71 respectively.

Ryde Pier Tramway

0.39 miles, 4ft. 8½ in. gauge, Pier section opened 29 Auguat 1864, horse traction. Extended 1.12 miles to St. John's Road Station on 7 August 1871. St.John's Road section closed 12 July 1880. Pier tramway, 0.39 miles, steam operated from 31 January 1881, horse from 1 November 1884, electric on third- rail system from 13 March 1886, petrol from November 1927. Closed 26 January 1969.

Horse traction: 6 open-top, double-deck cars and 2 single-deck closed cars. some possibly by Starbuck. Two single-deck trams were adapted to steam operation using coke. Electric traction: Two converted horse car plus four horse car trailers, all single-deck, 2 motor cars, one possibly both, by local firm of Pollards. Diesel traction: Nos.1-2, Drewry railcars with trailers built by the Southern Railway. Trailer No.4 built in 1871 is now at the Hull Museum.

Rye and Camber

c2.50 miles, 3ft. 0in. gauge. Opened 13 July 1895, closed September 1939. 2 Bagnall locomotives, Camber in green livery, Victoria in blue. Petrol locomotive by Kent Construction and Engineering Co. of Ashford in 1925. Dark green livery. 2 bogie coaches, one by Bagnall, one built locally.

Southampton Tramways Company

4.86 miles, 4ft.8½ in. gauge, horse traction, opened 5 May 1879, purchased by Southampton Corporation 1 July 1898. Rolling stock:- Nos.1-9,Bristol Wagon Company, 1879;Nos.10-20, Starbuck, 1879-82; Nos.21-27 North Metropolitan Tramways, Leytonstone, 1890-93 replacing Nos. 6,7,10,12,15,16, and Nos.28-31 Brush, 1896. All open-top, knifeboard seats. Last horse tram ran on 2 August 1901.

Southampton Corporation Tramways

13.70 miles, 4ft.8½ in. gauge, opened 22 January 1900, closed 31 December 1949. Livery crimson lake and cream, newer cars dark red and white. Some cars battleship grey in 1940-45.

Car Numbers	Type (as built)	Year Built	Builder	Seats	Truck(s)	Motors	Controllers
1- 20 (a)	Open top uncanopied	1900	Milnes	22/24	Brill 21E	Westinghouse 2 x 25hp	Westinghouse 5915
21- 29 (b)	Open top uncanopied	1901	Milnes	22/28	Brill 21E	Westinghouse 2 x 25hp	Westinghouse 5915
30- 37 (c)	Open top short canopy	1901	Milnes	24/33	Brill 21E	Westinghouse 2 x 25hp	Westinghouse 90?
38- 49 (d)	Open top uncanopied	1903	Hurst Nelson	24/24	Brill 21E	Westinghouse 2 x 25hp	Westinghouse 5915?
50- 51 (e)	Single-deck Demi-car	1906	SCT	26	Brill 21E	Westinghouse 2 x 25hp	Westinghouse 90
52- 55 (f)	Open top uncanopied	1908	SCT	24/24	Brill 21E	DK 25A 2 x 25hp	DK DB1 E
56- 59 (g)	Open top	1910	SCT	24/30	Brill 21E	DK 25A 2 x 25hp	DK DB1 E
60- 70 (h)	Open top	1910	SCT	24/30	Brill 21E	DK 10A2 2 x 32 hp	DK DB1 E
71- 73	Open top	1914	SCT	24/32	Brill 21E	DK 10A3 2 x 32 hp	DK DB1 K3
2(ii) (i)	Toastrack	1916	SCT	50	Brill 21E	Westinghouse 2 x 25hp	Westinghouse 5915
74 (j)	Open top	1917	SCT	24/42	Brill 21E	DK 10A3 2 x 32 hp	DK DB1 K3
51(ii) (k)	Balcony	1917	SCT	24/42	Brill 21E	DK 20A 2 x 40hp	DK DB1 K3
75- 80 (l)	Enclosed top deck	Bought 1918	ER&TCW	22/36	Brill 21E	DK 25A 2 x 25hp	DK DB1 C
81 (m)	Balcony	1918	SCT	28/44	Brill 21E	DK 20A 2 x 40hp	DK DB1 K3
82- 91	Balcony	1919	EE	22/38	Brill 21E	DK20A2 2 x 40hp	EE DB1 K3
5 cars (n)	Open top	1920-4	SCT	26/44	Brill 21E	DK20A 2 x 40hp	EE DB1 K3
11 cars (o)	Domed roof	1923-9	SCT	26/44	Brill 21E	BTH 265A 2 x 35/40hp	EE DB1 K3
92- 94 (p)	Domed roof	1926	SCT	24/44	Peckham P35	MV 101BR 2 x 40hp	EE DB1 K3
95-103 (p)	Domed roof	1926-9	SCT	24/44	Peckham P35	MV 101BXR 2 x 40hp	MV OK 9B
8 cars (q)	Domed roof	1929-30	SCT	21/38	Brill 21E	BTH265A 2 x 35/40hp	EE DB1 K3
104-109 (r)	Domed roof	1929-30	SCT	28/44	Peckham P35	MV 101BR 2 x 40hp	MV OK 9B
6 cars (s)	Domed roof	1930-1	SCT	24/36	Peckham P35	MV 101BR 2 x 40hp	MV OK 9B
1-2	Open Wagon		SCT	-	Brill 211E	Westinghouse 2 x 25hp	Westinghouse 5915
105E (t)	Welding car	1928	SCT	-	Brill 21E	Westinghouse 2 x 25hp	Westinghouse 5915

Notes

Four ex-horse cars, believed to be the four Brush cars Nos. 28-31, were used as trailers in 1900-01 and six of the first Milnes cars were equipped to haul them.

(a) Knifeboard seating on the upper-deck. Nos 4,6,7 rebuilt canopied 1913-1915, seating 22/32. Renumbered 40(iii), 34(ii), 36(ii), respectively in 1923. Nos 1, 3, 9-13, 15, 19, 20 renumbered 21(ii), 39(ii), 37(ii), 33(ii), 32(ii), 16(ii), 35(iii), 39(iii), 50(ii), 25(ii) respectively in 1923-25.

(b) Knifeboard seating on the upper-deck. Nos. 24, 26, 27, 29 rebuilt with extended canopies 1914, seating 22/32. No. 26 fitted DK DB1 controllers. No.22 converted to welding car 1928. Renumbered 105E.

(c) Garden seats on the upper-deck. Nos. 32, 34 rebuilt with balcony covers 1912. seating 22/38. Renumbered 30-31(ii) respectively in 1922. Nos. 30-31 fitted extended canopies, 1912, seating 22/37. Renumbered 32(ii), 34(ii) in 1922. Nos. 32(ii), 33, 34(ii), 35-37 rebuilt with extended canopies 1921-22. Nos. 32(ii), 33 fitted 32½hp DK 10A2 motors, No.34 40hp DK20A motors. Nos. 32(ii), 33, 35-37 renumbered 11(ii), 10(ii), 8(ii), 7(ii), 9(ii) in 1923 and further renumbered 3(iii), 2(iv), 5(iii), 1(iii), 4(ii) respectively in 1925. Nos. 34(ii), renumbered 6(ii) in 1923. All rebuilt as domed roof cars in 1929-30. See note q below.

(d) Knifeboard seating on the upper-deck. Nos. 38, 41, 42, 44, 49 canopied 1914-15, seating 24/28 or 24/32. Belived fitted with DK DB1 controllers. No. 45 rebuilt with top cover, 1917, seating 24/28. Rebuilt canopied open top, 1928, seating 24/32. Now, fitted DK DB1 K3 controllers, at the National Tramway Museum, Crich.

(e) Demi-cars with front entrances. Possibly built from Brush horse cars. No.50 converted to Welding car by 1921.

(f) Knifeboard seats on the upper deck. Nos.53-54 canopied 1922-23, seating 24/32. Fitted BTH motors.

(g) Knifeboard seats on the upper-deck. Canopies rebuilt from 1922, seating 24/34. No.59 on Brush truck when built. No.57 believed on experimental Barber radial truck c1910. Nos. 57-59 had BTH motors and Nos. 56, 59 DB1 K3 controllers.

(h) Knifeboard seating on the upper deck. Canopies rebuilt 1922-24, upper-deck seating 32, 34 or 36. No. 63 had UEC long wheelbase truck. At least Nos. 63-67 had Westinghouse controllers when built, by 1939 Nos. 60-62, 69-70 had EE DB1 K3 controllers and Nos. 63-67 probably MV OK 9B.

(i) Sold to Portsmouth in 1919.

(j) Initially built with front entrances. Rebuilt 1929 with domed roof, seating 24/38. Later fitted P35 truck and MV OK 9B controllers.

(k) Rebuilt 1929 with domed roof, seating 24/44.

(l) Ex-LCC B Class Nos. 135, 154, 161, 192, 198, 200 built 1903, The top deck covers were removed in 1922, and the lower saloons cut down, seating 22/35. DK DB1 K3 controllers latterly.

(m) Five side windows, rebuilt 1929 with domed roof.

(n) Five cars numbered 2(iii), 3-5(ii), 40(ii). No.40(ii) renumbered 1(ii) in 1923. Renumbered 10(iii), 11(iii), 9(iii), 8(iii), 7(iii) in 1925. These cars, now Nos. 7-11(iii), domed roof upper-decks in 1925. Nos. 8(iii), 9(iii), 11(iii) Peckham P35 trucks, 40hp MV 101B motors and MV OK 9B controllers.

(o) Eleven cars Nos, 12-15(ii), 16(iii), 17-20(ii), 22(ii), 37(iii). No. 13(ii) renumbered 31(iii) in 1944. Latterly some cars seated 24/44. Nos. 22(ii), 37(iii) had Peckham P35 trucks and MV OK 9B controllers. All, except No. 15(ii), had P35 trucks latterly. No.12(ii) was the prototype Domed roof car of 1923.

(p) No. 92 initially on rebuilt 21E truck. Nos. 92-94 initially had 35/40hp BTH 265A motors.

(q) Milnes 1901 cars Nos. 30-37, now renumbered 3(iii), 6(ii), 30(iii), 2(iv), 31(ii), 5(iii), 1(iii), 4(iii) rebuilt as short three window domed roof cars.

(r) Pullman Mark I

(s) Pullman Mark II. Nos. 21(iii), 23(ii), 25(iii), 32(iii), 35(ii), 50(ii).

(t) Ex No.22

37 of the 42 four window Domed Roof cars were sold to Leeds Corporation Tramways in 1949. Nos. 104-109 were renumbered 295, 294, 293, 290, 291 respectively. Nos. 50, 35, 32, 25, 23 were renumbered 296-300 respectively. Nos. 103, 95, 99, 92, 18, 10, 97, 101 were allocated numbers 301-307, 310 repectively, but did not enter service. Nos. 102, 19, 100, allocated Nos. 308, 311, 312 went direct to a farm near Farsley. Nos. 14, 21, 22, 37, 96, 98, not allocated Leeds numbers also went direct to Farsley. The trucks and equipment from the Farsley cars went to Kirkstall Road Works for spares or scrap. Nos. 7, 8, 12, 16, 17, 20, 74, 93, 94 were scrapped in Southampton.

Southampton Corporation No. 43, outside Shirley Depot. 5 April 1942.

(J.C.Gillham.

Eastbourne Tramways

0.9 miles, 2ft gauge. Opened 4 July 1954. Closed 14 September 1969. Operated by the MET Tramways Company. Livery green and cream.

Car Numbers	Type (as built)	Year Built	Builder	Seats	Truck(s)	Motors	Controllers
2	Open Top	1964	MET	35	MET EqW	2x3.75hp	DK DE1 Form B
3 (a)	Open Top	1952	LEC	20	LEC 4-wheel	2x2.25hp	Sharp
4	Open Boat single-deck	1961	MET	20	MET EqW	2x3.75hp	DK DB1 K33E
6 (b)	Toastrack	1954	MET	24	MET EqW	2x3.75hp	DK DB1 K3
7	Open Top	1958	MET	37	MET EqW	2x3.75hp	DK DB1 K3E
8	Open Top	1968	MET	43	MET EqW	2x3.75hp	DK DB1 K4
12	Single-deck saloon	1966	MET	20	MET EqW	2x3.75hp	DK DB1 K33E
23 (c)	Enclosed	1949	LEC	23 Children	LEC EqW	2x2.25hp	Sharp
225 (d)	Open Boat single deck	1950	LEC	12	LEC EqW	2x2.25hp	DB1 copy
226 (e)	Open Boat single deck	1954	LEC	12	LEC EqW	2X2.25hp	DB1 copy
238 (f)	Enclosed	1955	LEC	24	LEC EqW	2x2.25hp	DB1 copy
01 (g)	Tram Shop	1960	MET	—	LEC EqW	2x2.5hp	DB1 copy
02 (h)	Single deck works car	1952	MET	—	MET EqW	2x3.75hp	BTH B510

Notes
(a) Built as 15in gauge, regauged 1954 to 2ft gauge. Sold in 1963 to Mr Don Sorenson, Wilton, Connecticut, USA.
(b) Built as 15in gauge, rebuilt 1955 as open top seating 39 and 2ft gauge.
(c) 1957 sold to STMS, then MTPS, now in private ownership.
(d) Built as 15in gauge, rebuiltg 1952/3 slightly larger, regauged 1954 to 2ft gauge. Sold in 1963 to Mr Don Sorenson, Wilton, Connecticut, USA.
(e) Rebuilt 1960 as flat bed works car 01.
(f) Sold in 1963 to Mr Don Sorenson, Wilton, Connecticut, USA.
(g) Built as 226 (see note e) rebuilt as flat bed works car in 1960, then rebuilt in 1965 as the "Tram Shop".
(h) Commissioned in 1952 by Air Ministry as a battery operated 2ft gauge four wheel single deck car, the contract was cancelled in 1960 and the car used as a works car at Eastbourne, rebuilt 1968 with longer body anf equal wheel bogies.

Authorised Tramways Not Built

Hove and Worthing Electric Tramways Ltd.	Electric	4.81 miles	3ft. 6in.	1903.
Worthing Corporation Tramways.	Electric	7.90 miles	3ft. 6in.	1903.
Littlehampton Electric Tramways Co. (Volks)	Electric	1.0 miles	3ft. 6in.	1887.
Portsmouth & Hayling Island Light Railway.	Electric	3.9 miles	4ft. 7¾in	1905.
Gosport, Alverstoke & Bury Cross Tramways Co.	Horse	2.44 miles	3ft. 6in.	1889.
Fareham and Cosham, (Gosport, Fareham & Cosham Act)	Electric	5.0 miles*	4ft. 7½in.	1903.
Lyndhurts Electric Lighting & Traction Co. Ltd.	Electric	2.68 miles	4ft. 8½in.	1901.
Seaview and Bradley Harbour Steam Tramway.	Steam	1.90 miles	4ft. 8½in.	1882.
Ventnor and Bonchurch Tramway.	Steam	2.09 miles	4ft. 8½in.	1865.
Ventnor Inclinded Light Railway Company.	Cable	0.48 miles	5ft. 5in.	1898.
Carisbrooke, Newport & Parkhurst Tramways Co.	Horse	2.26 miles	?	1889.
Weymouth District Tramways Company.	Horse	0.96 miles	3ft. 0in.	1884.

Proposed Tramways Not Authorised

Eastbourne and Pevensey.	Steam	8.18 miles	3ft. 6in.	1884.
Brighton and South Coast.	Steam	9.30 miles	3ft. 6in.	1884.
Worthing Corporation.	Electric	8.90 miles	3ft. 6in.	1901.
Hove Corporation Tramways.	Electric	4.1 miles	3ft. 6in.	1903.
Hove, Worthing and District.	Electric	22.00 miles*	3ft. 6in.	1902.
Hampshire Tramways Co. Coaham-Waterlooville	Horse	3.49 miles	4ft. 7¾in.	1885.
Ryde & Seaview Light Railway Company.	Electric	2.70 miles	3ft. 6in.	1899.
Isle of Wight Tramways Co. Ltd., Freshwater.	Horse	2.90 miles	?	1879.
Isle of Wight Tramways Co. Ltd., Newport.	Horse	1.26 miles	?	1879.
Ventnor Tramway Company.	Steam	0.62 miles	4ft. 8½in.	1864.
Branksome Park & Swanage Light Railway Co.	Electric	13.25 miles	3ft. 6in.	1906.

*Approx Mileage.

Seaton and District Tramways

3.19 miles, 2ft 9in gauge. Opened 28 August 1970 (battery operation), 23 September 1973 (overhead collection). Operated by the MET Tramways Company. Livery various.

Car Numbers	Type (as built)	Year Built	Builder	Seats	Truck(s)	Motors	Controllers
2 (a)	Open Top	1964	MET	35	MET MxT	2x10hp	DK DE1 Form B
4 (b)	Open Boat single deck	1961	MET	20	MET MxT	2x10hp	DK DB1 K33E
6 (c)	Open Top	1954	MET	24	MET MxT	2x10hp	DK DB1 K3
7 (d)	Open Top	1958	MET	37	MET MxT	2x10hp	DK DB1 K3E
8 (e)	Open Top	1968	MET	43	MET MxT	2x10hp	DK DB1 K4
9-11	Open Top	2002	Bolton Trams	56	MET MxT	4x6hp	DK DB1 K33
12 (f)	Open Top	1966	MET	20	MET EqW	2x10hp	DK DB1 K33E
14 (g)	Single-deck saloon	1984	MET	27	MET MxT	2x10hp	GEC K10
16 (h)	Single-deck saloon	1992	MET	27	MET MxT	2x10hp	DK DB1 K4B
17 (i)	Single-deck crossbench	1988	MET	48	MET MxT	2x10hp	DK DE1 Form B
19 (j)	Single-deck saloon	1994	MET	20	MET MxT	2x10hp	DK DB1 K4
01 (k)	Gangers trailer	1960	MET	-	MET MxT	-	-
02 (i)	Tower works car	1952	MET	-	MET MxT	2X10hp	BTH B510
03	Welding trailer	1986	MET	-	MET EqW	-	-
04 (m)	Hydraulic hoist	1988	MET	-	MET EqW	-	-
05	Drop side wagon	1988	MET	-	MET 4W	-	-
06 (n)	Diesel tractor	2002	Kubota	-	-	Diesel	-

Notes

(a) Built as 2ft gauge, regauged 1970 to 2ft 9in.
(b) Built as 2ft gauge, regauged 1976 to 2ft 9in.
(c) Built as 15in gauge single deck toastrack, rebuilt 1955 as open top seating 39 and 2ft gauge, rebuilt 1962 with small lower deck saloons at each end, regauged 1976 to 2ft 9in and rebuilt 1990 removing lower saloons and replacing with crossbench seating.
(d) Built as 2ft gauge, regauged 1976 to 2ft 9in.
(e) Built as 2ft gauge, regauged 1970 to 2ft 9in. Rebuilt 1992 (lower salons removed and crossbench seating added).
(f) Built as 2ft gauge single deck enclosed car, regauged 1971 to 2ft 9in, rebuilt 1980 as open top seating 50, rebuilt 1999 with Feltham style ends seating 48.
(g) Built using the body of Metropolitan Electric Tramways car 94, built 1904.
(h) Built using the body of Bournemouth Corporation Tramways car 106, built 1921.
(i) Built for wheelchair bound passengers.
(j) Built using the body of Exeter Corporation Tramways car 19, built 1906.
(k) Originally built in 1954 as "Boat" 226 on 2ft gauge, rebuilt in 1960 as a flat bed works car, rebuilt 1965 as "Tram Shop", regauged 1973 to 2ft 9in and motors removed, rebuilt 1995 as gangers trailer.
(l) Commissioned in 1952 by Air Ministry as a battery operated 2ft gauge four wheel single deck car, the contract was cancelled in 1960 and the car used as a works car at Eastbourne. Rebuilt 1968, with longer body and equal wheel bogies, regauged to 2ft 9in in 1973, motors removed 1981, rebuilt 1992 after being damaged in a gale and motors replaced.
(m) Also called the "Bucket"
(n) Fitted with flanged metal guide wheels to allow it to run on the rails.

St Leonards Tramways

0.12 miles, 15 inch gauge. Opened 12 May 1951. Closed September 1951. Operated by the Lancaster Electrical Company. Livery green and cream.

Car Numbers	Type (as built)	Year Built	Builder	Seats	Truck(s)	Motors	Controllers
23	Enclosed	1949	LEC	23 Children	LEC EqW	2x2.25hp	Sharp
225	Open Boat single deck	1950	LEC	12	LEC EqW	2x2,25hp	DB1 copy

The sleepers that supported the track of 'Daddy-Long-legs' were still visible at low tide at Ovingdean on 3 January 1970.

(J.H.Price, National Tramway Museum.

Key to Abbreviations and Manufacturers

Aveling & Porter	—	Invicta Works, Rochester, Kent.
Bagnall	—	W.G. Bagnall & Co. Ltd., Stafford.
BEC	—	The British Electric Car Co. Ltd., Trafford Park, Manchester.
BCT	—	Brighton Corporation Tramways, Lewes Road Works, Brighton.
Brill	—	The J.G. Brill Company, Inc.. Philadelphia, USA.
Bristol Wagon	—	The Bristol Wagon & Carriage Works Ltd., Lawrence Hill, Bristol.
Brush	—	The Brush Electrical Engineering Co. Ltd., Loughborough.
BTH	—	The British Thomson-Houston Company Ltd., Rugby.
CEB	—	Compagnie Electrique Belge, Leige, Belgium.
DK	—	Dick, Kerr & Co. Ltd., Preston, Lancashire.
Dolter	—	Dolter Electric Traction Ltd., London E.C.
Drewry	—	Drewry Car Company.
E & H	—	Compagnie Electriqe et Hydraulique, Charleroi, Belgium.
EE	—	English Electric Co. Ltd., Preston, Lancashire.
Eq.W	—	Equal-wheel bogies.
ER&TCW	—	The Electric Railway & Tramway Carriage Works Ltd., Preston.
Falcon	—	Falcon Engine & Car Works, Loughborough. (Brush from 1889).
GE	—	The General Electric Company Inc. Schenectady, NY, USA.
GEC	—	General Electric Co. Ltd., Witton Works, Birmingham.
GGTC	—	Great Grimsby Street Tramways Co. Ltd., Victoria Street, Grimsby.
Greenwood & Batley	—	Greenwood & Batley Ltd., Albion Works, Leeds.
HN	—	Hurst Nelson & Company Ltd., Motherwell Scotland.
Kelsey	—	Kelsey's Motor Works, Hove. (Later Transport Motor Bodies Ltd.).
LEC	—	Lancaster Electrical Co., Brookhill Road, New Barnet.
LCC	—	London County Council Tramways, Charlton Works.
MET	—	Modern Electric Tramways Ltd., Brookhill Road, New Barnet
M & G	—	Mountain & Gibson Ltd., Bury, Lancashire.
Midland	—	Midland Railway Carriage & Wagon Co. Ltd., Shrewsbury, later Birmingham.
Milnes	—	Geo.F.Milnes & Co.Ltd., Hadley, Shropshire. (also at Birkenhead)
Milnes Voss	—	Milnes Voss & Co. Ltd., Cleveland Street, Birkenhead.
MV	—	Metropolitan Vickers Electrical Co. Ltd., Trafford Park, Manchester.
MxT	—	Maximum Traction bogies.
North Metropolitan	—	North Metropolitan Tramways Co., Leytonstone, London.
Peckham	—	Peckham Truck & Engineering Co. Ltd.
PCT	—	Portsmouth Corporation Tramways, North End Depot.
SCT	—	Southampton Corporation Tramways, Portswood Works.
Siemens	—	Siemens Brothers Dynamo Works Ltd. Stafford
Starbuck	—	Starbuck Car & Wagon Co. Ltd., Birkenhead.
Tilling Stevens	—	Tilling Stevens Co. Ltd., London.
UEC	—	United Electric Car Company Ltd., Strand Road, Preston.
Westinghouse	—	Westinghouse Electric Co. Ltd., Trafford Park, Manchester.
Wilkinson	—	William Wilkinson & Co. Ltd., Pemberton, Wigan.

Acknowledgements and Sources

This book is based on Chapter 10, The Coastal Chain, of Great British Tramway Networks by W.H.Bett and J.C.Gillham (Fourth Edition, LRTL, 1962), with additional information from more recent books and articles in Tramway Review. Other periodicals consulted included The BET Gazette, Light Railway and Tramway Journal, Modern Tramway, Modern Transport, Railway Magazine and Tramway World.

Thanks are due to Rosie Thacker, Librarian, and Glynn Wilton, Photographic Officer, at the John Price Memorial Library at the National Tramway Museum, for their help with source material and locating photographs. Thanks are due to J. Allpress, G.B.Claydon, E.Elliston, F.P.Groves, N.A.Kellett, M.Petch and D.Voice for additional information.

The tramcar fleet lists were compiled by R.J.S. Wiseman with the valued assistance of F.P.Groves and D.Voice. The publishers would be pleased to receive any additional information for possible publication in Tramway Review.

The Pevensey, Portsmouth, Southampton and Poole maps have been drawn by J.C.Gillham. Other maps have been drawn by R.A.Smith and are based on those originally drawn by J.C.Gillham for Brighton and the Isle of Wight, W.J.Wyse for Shoreham, N.A.Kellett for Worthing, E. Beddard for Hastings and F.J.Roche for Bournemouth. The area map is based on that by J.C.Gillham.

Photographs have been reproduced by kind permission of R.Brook, A.W.Brotchie, C.Carter, J.C.Gillham, P.Hewson, J.H.Meredith, D Voice and M.G.C.W. Wheeler. Also the Science Museum, Science and Society Picture Library, London, and the National Tramway Museum, Crich.

Bibliography — General
Great British Tramway Networks, by W.H.Bett and J.C.Gillham, (Light Railway Transport League, 4th. Edition 1962).
The Definitive Guide to Trams (including Funiculars), in the British Isles, by David Voice (Adam Gordon, 2001).
The Directory of British Trams, by Keith Turner (Patrick Stephens, 1996).
A Regional History of the Railways of Great Britian, Volume 2, Southern England, by H.P.White (Phoenix House, 1961).
What Colour was that Tram, by David Voice (Author, 4th Edition 1998)
Bournemouth
The History of The Tramways of Bournemouth and Poole, by R.C.Anderson, A.M.Inst.T (LRTL, 1964).
Bournemouth and Poole Tramways, by Roy C.Anderson (Middleton Press, 1995).
Brighton
The Brighton Corporation Tramways, by Ronald M. Harmer (in *Tramway Review* Nos. 44-47, 1965-66).
Brighton Tramways, by Robert J. Harley (Middleton Press, 1992).
Brighton and Shoreham Tramway
The Brighton and Shoreham Tramway, by R.M.Harmer (in Tramway Review Nos. 42-43 1965).
Eastbourne
Seaton and Eastbourne Tramways, by Robert J.Harley (Middleton Press, 1996).
Eastbourne Tramways, by Bob Ellison (in *Eastbourne Local Historian* No.128, 2003).

Gosport and Fareham
The Tramways of Portsmouth, by S.E.Harrison (LRTL., 1955).
Gosport and Horndean Tramways, by Martin Petch (Middleton Press, 1997).

Hastings
Hastings Tramways, by G.L.Gundry (in Tramway Review Nos.89-92, 1977).
Hastings Tramways, by Robert J.Harley (Middleton Press, 1993).

Hellingly
The Hellingly Hospital Tramway, by Peter A. Harding (Author, 1989)

Hythe Pier
Pier Railways and Tramways, by Keith Turner (The Oakwood Press, 1999).

Portsmouth, Portsdown and Horndean
The Tramways of Portsmouth, by S.E. Harrison (LRTA, 1955).
Portsmouth's Tramways, by Martin Petch (Middleton Press, 1996).
Gosport and Horndean Tramways, by Martin Petch (Middleton Press 1997).

Ryde Pier
Pier Railways and Tramways, by Keith Turner (The Oakwood Press, 1999).
Ryde Pier Tramway, by J.H.Price (in *Modern Tramway,* December 1966).

Rye and Camber
The Rye and Camber Tramway, by C.Judge (The Oakwood Press, 1995).

Seaton
Seaton and Eastbourne Tramways, by Robert J. Harley (Middleton Press, 1996).
Next Stop Seaton, by David Jay and David Voice (Adam Gordon 2003).

Selsey
Branch Line to Selsey, by Vic Mitchell and Keith Smith (Middleton Press, 1983).
The Selsey Tram, by David Bathurst (Phillimore, 1992).

Southampton
Southampton Corporation Tramways, by J.C.Gillham (in *Modern Tramway,* March 1941).
Southampton Tramways by Martin Petch (Middleton Press, 1994).

Volks Railway
The Inventive Genius of Magnus Volk, by R.M. Harmer (in *Tramway Review* No.44, 1965).
Volks Railways, by Alan A. Jackson (in *Modern Tramway* July-August 1963).
Magnus Volk of Brighton, by Conrad Volk (Phillimore Press, Chichester 1971).

Worthing
The Tramways of Worthing, by N.A.Kellett   (in *Tramway Review* Nos. 143,145-46, 1990-1991).

Back Cover
Above   Southampton 45 at Wakebridge waiting to leave for Crich, Town End, on
             1 September 1999.   (R.J.S. Wiseman
Below   Portmouth 84, converted from a horse tram, was saved by the
             Corporation and is now at the Hampshire Museum in Basingstoke.
                                                    (J.C. Gillham
Inside Back Cover
Above   The ride down Portsdown Hill to Cosham on the upper deck of a
             Horndean tram must have been exhilerating. The greater part of the
             background has been built on since this card was published early last
             century.   (Tucks card, courtesy A.W. Brotchie.
Below   A ride from Seaton alongside the River Axe can offer a similar
             experience today. Open top trams Nos.7 and 8 are seen at Colyton
             terminus in May 2002.
                                            (David Voice

Published 2004 by Light Rail Transit Association, 13a The Precinct, Brokbourne, Hants EN10 7HX.
Printed by Spectrum Print Direct, Leamore Lane, Walsall WS2 7DQ. Tel: (01922) 428267